To Carla,
12/18
Thank you so
much for always
being a
and know
your story &
your own
love,
[signature]

FAITH
THROUGH
THE FOG

*A story of hope, courage,
perseverance, and healing*

LISA FRANK, TH.B

Faith Through The Fog is a compelling personal account that is sure to ignite a paradigm shift in the way you view mental illness. This writing exemplifies perseverance, hope, and demonstrates how to have faith in God in spite of tragedy. You will gain confidence in the knowledge that ALL things, as promised in Romans 8:28, are working out for your benefit.

In Loving Memory of

Sean Ragin
July 27, 1976–April 5, 2008

My dear nephew Sean lived his life being kind to others and making a positive impact on both the young and the old. He was wise beyond his years and had a smile that could warm the saddest of hearts. His smile and encouragement gave me the strength to keep moving forward during difficult times.

Matthew Warren
"The Compassionate Warrior"
1986–April 5, 2013

Matthew fought the good fight of faith as he touched and encouraged many who were in emotional pain. It's been said that "Mathew had the ability to walk in a room and identify the person who was in emotional pain."

Nicole Dunlap
July 22, 1997–July 30, 2015

Nicole was a gifted and talented writer who touched the lives of many through poetry and screenwriting. She created short films and videos. She was widely known for her acting, singing, and spoken word. Although Nikki (as we fondly called her) lost her battle with mental illness, she lives on through her organ donation to the Sharing Network of New Jersey.

Whilamena L. Abernathy
November 22, 1952–May 3, 2016

To my loving sister who was my rock throughout my life. She taught me many things in life about understanding people and managing relationships. She was always there in times of crisis. Through her death, she taught me that we must take care of our physical bodies because the symptoms that medical conditions produce can also affect and challenge our mental capacity. A favorite saying that we shared was, "Keep it moving."

Dedication

Pastor Rick and Kay Warren
(Matthew's parents)

For first acknowledging that Matthew was ill; having the courage to admit it; then for seeking America's best doctors, medications, counselors, and prayers. Your family was courageous and used mightily by God in spite of the dense fog that was before you from Matthew's cradle to adult years. You both have worked diligently to break the stigma of mental illness and highlight the awareness that the brain, just as the rest of the body, can break down. For your book *Purpose Driven Life* which pointed out that I have an obligation to share my story because it is the gift that God has given me to serve Him and His people.

Frances and Angie Dunlap
(Nicole's mother and sister)

For the support you provided for Nicole in the best way that you knew how, and for your efforts to encourage treatment. You loved her with a courageous and unconditional love in spite of the challenges associated with her mental illness.

Acknowledgments

Many thanks to my daughter, Jélissa, and son, Oscar, who have taken the time to share their heart and experiences that are included in this work. Thank you for the many years you have shared me with those who I've been destined to counsel and minister to. For loving and forgiving me in spite of the many challenges you endured, and for remaining stable in the midst of the fog of mental illness. My deceased mother, Hattie Abernathy, who taught me the importance of bearing the burdens of others and to persevere through challenges until the goal was accomplished. To my dad, Willie Abernathy, who taught me that there is a solution to every problem and, if I wrestle with it long enough, I will find it. To my cousin Regina Hall-Barbour for her prayers that avail much, encouragement, and for allowing God to use her to push me toward publishing this book.

To my current Pastor, Dr. Dharius Daniels (Author of *Re-Presenting Jesus*) and First Lady Shameka Daniels who have contributed tremendously to my understanding of what it takes to live a successful Christian life. This has impacted my perspective on my call to parenting, financial stewardship, natural and spiritual vocations. Thank you for teaching me how to develop and manage healthy relationships and how to detach from the drama in my life. They have both been a wonderful example in more ways than I can express. I appreciate the way in which you encourage Christians not to be ashamed of the need to seek professional help. You have done so while ministering and by being transparent about your own submission to therapeutic support. Your Friday Night

Uncensored sessions have exposed my limited understanding of the correct approach to dating and selecting a life partner.

To my former Pastor Dr. A. R. Bernard, Sr. (Author of *Four Things Women Want From A Man*) and Pastor Karen Bernard for 18 years of tutelage, and the many principles that I have learned and passed on to others in this struggle. I have never forgotten that boundaries are how far you are willing to let others go, and limitations are how far I am willing to go. Thank you for holding me up spiritually, financially and otherwise during times when life happened, as well as when I fell short because of my own lack of wisdom.

To my special friends Jamel and Trilbie who have supported close friends in their efforts to live with Bipolar Disorder; and for sharing your experiences of loving someone with Bipolar, and other mental illnesses to help me. Thank you to all of my other close friends and relatives who have prayed for me. You all have taken the time to encourage me for the past thirty-five years through my personal struggles and various shifts in my life. If I have forgotten anyone, I ask that you charge it to my head and not my heart because my gratitude for the ways people have impacted my life runs deep.

Sincere thanks to Shaun Saunders of Godzchild Publications for the initial edits, and Tessywriter at Fiverr for the final edits. Thanks to www.bookclaw.com for formatting this book and for the final cover design. Special thanks to my Christian Life, Inc. mentors Bridget Burns (Founder) and Dr. Marsha Clarke (Director of Training) for training me as a Christian Life Coach. Thank you both for the opportunity to publish a synopsis of this book in Again I Rise:

The Women's Compilation Project; and their friendship.

Special Thanks

I found Thea Stevenson on Upwork to do the cover of this book. She did an outstanding job manifesting the vision that I had in my mind which was the inspiration for the final design. Her design was also used for promotional material.

Foreword

Faith Through The Fog is written by a person who has superseded our relationship as cousins and morphed into becoming the sister I never had. As counselors, we had the privilege of working together at several agencies, as she impacted many lives with her gifts. I have often joked and told her that when I grow up, I want to be like her, even though we are only one year apart. I have watched Lisa go through some of the most painful events of her life as she encountered the physical and emotional abuse from being the "Joseph of her family of origin." She endured a tumultuous marriage, homelessness with a husband and children, and the painful events leading up to the death of her mother and sister. There were also the dark symptoms of mental illness, and perpetual cycles of financial deprivation.

During the years that she walked through the valley of the shadow of death, I was honored to have a front row seat while watching God shepherd her through it all. He taught her life-changing lessons of fearing no evil. I was always amazed by the ways God would grant her favor, which became the nickname I gave her, as she has traveled to several countries, had the privilege of sitting at the feet of people of influence, getting her son into prestigious boarding schools, and many more blessings that are too many to name. I was always in awe as she would apply God's word to every struggle of her life, and applied the principles that she had learned from sitting under the leadership of Pastor A.R Bernard, Sr.

She walks in wisdom and insight beyond her years, while being an established counselor second to none. This book is a spiritually based therapeutic coaching tool to walk anyone who is challenged with getting through the fog of their struggles in life. I applaud her courage to speak openly about mental illness to churches and crossing cultural boundaries. I am confident that her transparency will set you and those you love and interact with free.

Regina Hall-Barbour

Author of *Saved, Single and Seeking to be Satisfied*

Contents

Dedication 6

Acknowledgments 8

Special Thanks 10

Foreword 13

Preface 19

Introduction to the Fog 22

Spared For A Purpose 25

Called For Such A Time As This 28

A Few Alarming Facts and Descriptions of Mental Disorders 34

Kay Jamison, Ph. D. 40

You Can't Conquer What You Won't Admit, So Let's Face It 43

Grieving the Loss of Good Health 47

Why Not Meds? 54

Therapy 59

Mood Swings 64

Decisions 68

Jélissa's Story 73

Oscar's Story 77

Money and Bipolar 82

Relationships and Bipolar 86

Employment and Mental Illness 89

Education and Mental Illness 93

Depression 97

Wisdom in Disclosure 101

Chris Biehn's Story 105

Suicide 109

Angie's Story 113

A Peaceful Fog 118

Self-Care 121

Health Check 129

Conclusion 138

References 142

Resources 143

Notes 144

Biography 145

Preface

The goal of this book is to help individuals and their families to better understand, acknowledge, seek help, and be healed of the hurt stemming from both mental illness and the stigma tied to it. My prayer is that you will be encouraged and motivated to courageously move through the fog of mental illness to living a successful life. This book will take a hard stance against the barriers that prevent individuals from getting the help they need for themselves, family members, or friends. This journey will be laced with stories where I have changed some of the names and places to respect the privacy of people whom I have counseled over the years.

This book can apply to any category of mental illness, but my primary experience and study has been with Bipolar (Manic Depression) and Depression Disorders. I have completed extensive coursework that is necessary to become certified as an addictions counselor. Much of that coursework included a focus on Mentally Ill and Chemically Addicted (MICA), other addictions, grief, and HIV/AIDS counseling. My counseling experience has been with individuals in correctional facilities, family counseling practices, methadone clinics, and privately. That work has lead people to identify mental illness in themselves, family members, intimate relationships, friendships and associates as well as ways to successfully manage it.

Along with the opportunity to educate people on ways to manage mental illness, I have obtained connections with resources and other agencies for consistent support. I strongly encourage group therapy because its purpose is to gain normalcy from others that are experiencing the same challenges. The devil will attempt to separate us from others by telling us that no one understands, but we have to fight and break out of that thinking knowing that there is no one who knows exactly what we are going through but sharing similarities of our issues helps a great deal. God gives us relationships for a season or a lifetime, but most of all, for a purpose. John Donne stated that no man is an island to himself because we are interconnected and cannot grow or heal in isolation.

Introduction to the Fog

The unfolding of what it means to move through the fog of mental illness became clear to me while I traveled from Virginia back to New Jersey in a complete fog. This was a fog unlike any that I had ever experienced before. We headed to Virginia early that Sunday morning to bring my son back to school following Christmas break. There was a freezing rain alert, so the roads did not present favorable conditions. I was in a unique situation because I had just begun a new job so I did not have the luxury of waiting until the inclement weather to pass. This would otherwise have been a six-hour trip each way, but it turned into eight and a half hours each way. I had to embrace this arduous journey at a timid, snail's pace believing God for traveling mercy to reach our destination and make it back home safely. My daughter was with me as I drove home from Virginia through the fog but was tired, and went to sleep. This gave me an opportunity to consider and gain clarity about the ways in which the fog related to mental illness and what God wanted me to convey in this book.

The minute I started driving through that intense fog, I contemplated many scenarios that would offer some control over what was before me. However, I was forced to embrace the realization that none of the ideals in my mind could conquer or alter the reality of my situation. If you are the person experiencing the neurochemical imbalance (mental illness), or are the spouse, child, family member, landlord, tenant, neighbor, pastor, teacher, boss, or co-worker connected to the person with the neurochemical imbalance, you have contemplated alternative scenarios. However, at some point, you were confronted with the realization that you had to accept that you would not escape this fog. You also had to accept that you had no control over it.

So I braced myself and proceeded, but not without giving consideration to all of the bad things that could happen along the way as a result of the current conditions. From whatever position you find yourself in, I am quite sure that you have also braced yourself but agonized over things that could impact you as you moved through the fogginess of mental illness. Please know that by faith, and looking through it at God, you can be victorious. You can experience healing in whatever way God chooses to heal, so that you are enabled to live a balanced life.

Spared For A Purpose

"You intended to harm me, but God intended it for good to accomplish what is now being done, the saving of many lives."
(Genesis 50:20 NIV)

At age four, while crossing the street in front of my house, I was struck by a hit and run drunken driver. It was a traumatic brain injury that left part of my brain lying on the sidewalk. My parents were told that I wouldn't survive, and if I did, I would be a vegetable. My praying grandfather (Pastor Allen Parks) and my praying aunts rushed to my bedside. They anointed me with oil and believed God for my healing. I have spent my entire life listening to them testify about how God brought me out of the coma in 3 days and how I WALKED out of the hospital in 13 days. They always followed up with how my head was shaved bald, but now my hair was long and thick, and they emphasized how I always excelled in school and how God was to be glorified.

At age 20, I was being treated for Ulcerative Colitis and given a sulfa-based medication. At that time, I did not know that I had G6-PD Blood Deficiency and was allergic to sulfa. As a result, I ended up in the hospital with a mild form of Stevens-Johnson syndrome for three weeks. It begins with flu-like symptoms, followed by a painful red or purplish rash on the entire body that spreads and blisters. Then the entire top layer of the affected skin dies and sheds. The enemy meant it for evil to take my life, but God meant it for good. Five years earlier, during a fight with one of my siblings, I received second-degree burns from hot coffee that was tossed in my face and settled on my chest. By the time I reached the hospital, my chest was filled with blisters. The physician ripped off the blisters, bandaged me up and sent me home. I lived with the physical scars on my chest for all those years, often wondering whether I would be repulsive to my future spouse. But God!!! During the Stevens-Johnson episode, when my skin completed the shedding process, the physical scars from the burns went away.

I never understood why my family always made such a big deal about my recovery from the accident. Nor did I fully embrace the totality of what God did, or why He spared my life. After much resistance, I have decided to share in this book all that the enemy meant for evil and trust God that it will turn the lives of many around for good. What we are is God's gift to us, and what we do with ourselves is our gift to Him.

Called For Such A Time As This

"For if you remain silent at this time, relief and
deliverance for the Jews will arise from another
place, but you and your father's family will
perish. And who knows but that you have come to
your royal position for such a time as this?"
(Esther 4:14 NIV)

A calling is a gift and burden (the thing that keeps you up at night) colliding. January 2003, my husband, children and I moved to our new home after being in transition for three years. During this arduous wilderness experience, we lived in seven (the number of completion) different locations. This wilderness experience transpired after selling our first home in May 2000. It was a long journey that taught me a great deal about life and people. I learned the reality of the lesson that my mother taught me over the years, which was that you find out who your true friends are when you are down and out.

Shortly after settling in, I re-entered the field of addictions and began working at a local methadone clinic as a Substance Abuse Counselor. I was very happy to be in our newly refurbished home after the journey. This was evidenced by the tears that began to flow when I removed my refrigerator magnet collection from the box and strategically placed them on **MY** refrigerator. It signified that the journey was finally over but, little did I know, a new one with many roots from the past would begin to unfold.

I have always loved wallpaper and borders and often stayed up late nights putting them up, and because I worked around the corner from home, I would cut pieces, prepare the glue and run home during my 30-minute lunch break to continue the process. One month later, I had my son's fifth birthday party, and many of my old friends were in attendance with their children. Everyone was astonished by the fact that my home was fully decorated and commented over and over that they could not believe we only lived there for a month. Unbeknownst to us, this was not something to be commended; however, this is identified as abnormal compulsions and mania. Now there are people who remodel and decorate their home in a month's time, but it is with painters, contractors, help from family members and friends. It is not generally done in a month alone while working a full-time job, caring for a spouse and two small children. This was a frequent response to days of sleepless nights where I would stay up redecorating, searching the internet, following ideas that weren't ideal decisions led by God, talking on the phone, or emailing friends. I would then go to sleep after my manic activity for one or two hours and get up energized as if I had had a full night's sleep. This behavior was deemed as productive and led to grandiose thinking that I was a superwoman of all superwomen. My friends and I marveled at what I was accomplishing, but none of us had the insight to realize that this behavior was a sign of a bigger issue.

In my role at the methadone clinic, I was responsible for individual and group counseling. Some of the therapeutic techniques that I used to help my clients involved self-assessments which identified treatment issues. I often completed the assessments myself so that I could see the limitations and strengths of the tool as well as what completing it was like from a client's perspectives. March of that year, I completed an assessment that outlined some struggles that I was facing, and was also able to pinpoint the onset of those struggles. Many experts have said that many people have the gene of mental illness lying dormant in their brain; however, it oftentimes remains dormant until a traumatic event or a traumatic brain injury takes place.

After evaluating certain behaviors, I realized that it was around the time when my older sister Mena (as we fondly called her) and her boyfriend of a few years were in a serious car wreck on Christmas day that these symptoms began to surface. These telltale signs were the pressure speech and speaking rapidly, decreased need for sleep, inability to stay in one place at a time, and mismanagement of money. The accident took place just blocks from my oldest sister's apartment building, when their car spun on the snowy road and wrapped around a utility pole. I was thirteen years old, and I can still remember sitting at first in the back seat of my parent's car, watching my parents hurl questions at each other about this tragedy that happened to some unknown person. I sat in the emergency room, and all of the parents were in tears. I finally mustered up the nerve to ask my oldest sister what happened and why we were there. Shortly after that conversation, her boyfriend's parents were escorted down the hallway, and I heard the screams of his mother when the reality within her cry told me that the accident had claimed her son's life. My sister's boyfriend was a man who I held dear to my heart and considered to be a big brother.

I was now experiencing my first major loss, and the hospitalization with my sister being comatose and barely clinging to life for nearly a month following that accident. I was thirteen, and my sister was hospitalized for close to five months, but my mother had to return to work shortly after the accident. At thirteen, in those days, I was not of legal age to visit my sister. Every evening, I had a different story for my mother about how I evaded the security guards in order to visit with my sister and monitor her progress. All of the photos of my sister's boyfriend were destroyed in an effort to protect her from the devastating loss once she regained consciousness. For reasons unknown to me, we never attended his funeral, and that further impacted the loss since he was like a big brother to me. After all, he gave me my first amethyst birthstone ring and made me laugh all of the time. I genuinely admired them both, as I often recollected the joy on their faces and the stunning fur jacket that my sister was wearing when they journeyed out the afternoon of the accident. Mena was hurt badly, and she had a long road toward recovery from this tragic accident.

As I chronicled the onset of my illness, I identified this as the trauma that greatly impacted and shaped the thirty years prior to being diagnosed and treated for Bipolar Disorder. The depression I experienced in May of 2003 was a pivotal point that I didn't see as anything but a curse; however, throughout this writing, I will point out the many experiences and blessings that have led to me seeing my way through the fog of mental illness to success. I am, thereby, venturing to utilize my experiences, education and God's help to guide you through your fog to the successful management of mental illness through faith in Him.

The Bible tells us that when we are comforted, we are to strengthen and encourage others with our testimonies. I pray that as you read through these pages, your faith will grow in the realization that God is with you, knows your struggles and can give you the stamina as you persevere. I believe that only God can take what was meant for evil and bless you to live a life that is purpose driven. You can live on purpose and be a demonstration of God's ability to turn your mess into a message. He never comforts us to be comfortable but so that we can comfort others. I will continue to share other parts of my story and outcomes in various degrees as it relates to each chapter.

God, if it is in Your best interest to remove this suffering, please do so. But if it fulfills Your purpose, that's what I want, too.

A Few Alarming Facts and Descriptions of Mental Disorders

"My People are destroyed for lack of knowledge."
(Hosea 4:6)

It is important to note that The National Institute of Mental Health (NIMH) in 2010 estimated that 7.7 million Americans have schizophrenia and bipolar disorder. This was approximately 3.3% of the US population when combined. Of these, approximately 40% of the individuals with schizophrenia and 51% of those with bipolar are untreated in any given year, according to NIMH.

The consequences of non-treatment are devastating and can lead to homelessness, episodes of violence, murder, victimization, and suicide. These consequences, in turn, translate into fiscal costs, federal benefits, incarceration, and other related costs.

This book is not a tool to be used for diagnosis, or to determine a course of treatment options, but I believe it is necessary to highlight and describe a few of the prevalent disorders. There are numerous classes of mental illnesses, but this is a list of the most common and their descriptions.

Anxiety & Panic

Current research suggests that one in ten Americans suffer from anxiety that disrupts their ability to function. Anxiety disorders are manifested in many different types of physical, psychological, and behavioral symptoms. Specific types of Anxiety disorders include: Obsessive-Compulsive Disorder, Generalized Anxiety Disorder, Panic Disorder, Social Phobia, and Post-Traumatic Stress Disorder.

Psychosis

The transition from adolescence to adulthood carries the heightened risk of emerging symptoms that may lead to the onset of a psychiatric illness such as schizophrenia. It is of utmost value to understand that psychosis is a break from reality, and the individual is unavailable for help until the medication has stabilized them. Symptoms that indicate potential risk of early psychosis can be non-specific and may include changes in the following:

- *thinking and ideations*
- *perception*
- *emotion regulation*
- *cognition*
- *social interactions*

Mood Disorders

Mood disorders, including depression and bipolar disorder, are characterized by extreme mood states that are not controllable and which interfere with daily living. Depressed persons may feel sad, distressed, and hopeless—even though there is no reason for them to feel that way. People with bipolar disorder may experience abnormally high energy and an elevated sense of mood and self that interferes with their ability to make reasonable choices. Mood disorders are common and treatable medical illnesses.

Bipolar Disorders

Bipolar disorder, also known as manic-depressive disorder, affects millions of people each year. Those who live with this disorder have incredible highs (mania) and disabling lows (depression). According to The National Institute of Mental Health, Bipolar Disorder affects more than 2 million American adults. There are several types of bipolar and related disorders. For each type, the exact symptoms of bipolar disorder can vary from person to person. Bipolar I and bipolar II disorders also have additional specific features that can be added to the diagnosis based on your particular signs and symptoms.

Criteria for Bipolar Disorder

The Diagnostic and Statistical Manual of Mental Disorders (DSM-5), published by the American Psychiatric Association, lists criteria for diagnosing bipolar and related disorders. This manual is used by mental health providers to diagnose mental conditions and by insurance companies to reimburse for treatment.

Diagnostic criteria for bipolar and related disorders are based on the specific type of disorder.

Bipolar I Disorder

You've had at least one manic episode. The manic episode may be preceded by or followed by hypomanic or major depressive episodes. Mania symptoms cause significant impairment in your life and may require hospitalization or trigger a break from reality (psychosis).

Bipolar II Disorder

You've had at least one major depressive episode lasting at least two weeks and at least one hypomanic episode lasting at least four days, but you've never had a manic episode. A hypomanic episode is characterized by elevated mood plus three other symptoms, such as irritable mood plus pressured speech, inflated self-esteem, grandiosity, and decreased need for sleep. Major depressive episodes or the unpredictable changes in mood and behavior can cause distress or difficulty in all areas of your life.

Cyclothymic Disorder

You've had at least two years or one year in children and teenagers of numerous periods of hypomania symptoms (less severe than a hypomanic episode) and periods of depressive symptoms (less severe than a major depressive episode). During that time, symptoms occur at least half the time and never go away for more than two months. Symptoms cause significant distress in important areas of your life.

Other types

These include, for example, bipolar and related disorders due to another medical condition such as Cushing's disease, multiple sclerosis, or stroke. Another type is called substance and medication-induced bipolar and related disorder.

Bipolar II disorder is not a milder form of bipolar I disorder but a separate diagnosis. While the manic episodes of bipolar I disorder can be severe and dangerous, individuals with bipolar II disorder can be depressed for longer periods, which can cause significant impairment.

Kay Jamison, Ph. D.

"Describes what it is like to have bipolar."

"There is a particular kind of pain, elation, loneliness, and terror involved in this kind of madness. When you're high, it's tremendous. The ideas and feelings are fast and frequent like shooting stars, and you follow them until you find better and brighter ones. Shyness goes, the right words and gestures are suddenly there, and the power to captivate others becomes a felt certainty. There are interests found in uninteresting people. Sensuality is pervasive, and the desire to seduce and be seduced is irresistible. Feelings of ease, intensity, power, well-being, financial omnipotence and euphoria pervade one's marrow. But somewhere, this changes. The fast ideas are too fast, and there are far too many; overwhelming confusion replaces clarity. Memory goes. Humor and absorption on friend's faces are replaced by fear and concern. Everything previously moving with the grain is now against it ... you are irritable, angry, frightened, uncontrollable, and emerged totally in the blackest caves of the mind. You never knew those caves were there. It will never end, for madness carves its own reality.

"It goes on and on, and finally there are only others' recollections of your behavior ... your bizarre, frantic, aimless behaviors ... for mania has at least some grace in partially obliterating memories. What then after the medication, psychiatrist, despair, depression, and overdose? All those incredible feelings to sort through. Who is being too polite to say what? Who knows what? What did I do? Why? And most hauntingly, when will it happen again? Then, too, are the bitter reminders ... medicine to take, resent, forget, take, resent, and forget, but always to take. Credit cards revoked, bounced checks to cover, explanations due at work, apologies to make, intermittent memories (what did I do?), a ruined marriage. And always, when will it happen again? Which of my feelings are real? Which of the me's is me? The wild impulsive chaotic, energetic, and crazy one? Or the shy, withdrawn, disparate, suicidal, doomed, and tired one? Probably a bit of both, hopefully much that is neither. Virginia Woolf, in her dives and climbs, said it all, 'How far do our feelings take their colour from the dive underground? I mean, what is the reality of any feeling?'"

Father, in Your precious name Jesus, I pray that You will provide us with safe environments and people that You have destined to help with this. Lord, I pray that You will swiftly remove anyone that sets out to monopolize, manipulate, or abuse us in this process. Thank You for equipping the body of Christ to bear each other's burdens. Give us the right words to minister to each other in times when support is needed. In Jesus' name.

You Can't Conquer What You Won't Admit, So Let's Face It

"Confess your faults one to another, and pray one
for another that ye may be healed,"
(James 5:16 KJV)

I was 40 when diagnosed, and that crisis was during daylight savings time, as both spring and fall (Daylight Savings Time) tends to cause an imbalance in people with Bipolar Disorder. That spring, I began waking up and crying for no reason every morning. I loved my job but was having a difficult time getting ready to venture into work for weeks. One morning, I was speaking to my friend, Jamel, who at that point had known me for thirteen years, rocked my two babies, and sheltered me when we were homeless. I finally broke down and told her what I was going through. She had had a friend years prior to that who had Bipolar Disorder and stated that my symptoms sounded similar. She strongly recommended that I make an appointment to be evaluated. I also shared it with my friend, Trilbie, who at that point had known me for nine years. We met rocking our daughters Alexandrea and Jélissa in the lobby of church when there was no nursery. Trilbie also had a great deal of knowledge and experience with the disorder and witnessed friends and their families endure some debilitating and fatal outcomes as a result. She concurred with Jamel's advice to seek professional help since this crying episode had lasted for more than a month.

I had experienced bouts of severe depression throughout my life beginning, as previously stated, at age thirteen. I described this life as being one that mimics the song's lyrics, "The tears of a clown, when no one is around." I say this because I would make every effort to be happy and make others happy, but I would often go in private places and cry for hours. I often contemplated suicide and proceeded to cut my wrists a few times. During those times I was cutting at my wrist, I felt like I just wanted to die. Praise God, that during suicidal ideations I always thought about how much pain it would cause my parents and others if I ended my life. That resulted in me simply wanting someone to acknowledge my despair and help me feel better. Afterwards, I would feel so embarrassed, so I would hide my wrists from everyone until the scars faded.

For years, I battled with financial troubles and never was able to save or finish things that I started because of mania, mood swings and depression. I often went for days without sleep, and then would eventually encounter what is called crashing. When the cycle of crashing happens, the person becomes extremely depressed and cannot function. Once diagnosed with Bipolar Disorder, I went to counseling and began the process of finding the right medication. Medication management was difficult because I have a high sensitivity to many medications. I had spent many years staying up late at night. I was obsessed with fixing the house when I was frustrated and unable to fix other things in my life, so I had to learn how to rest and sleep again. I desperately wanted to fix my marriage and finances but didn't realize that my difficulty applying God's Word to those areas was rooted in this illness. When manic, I would stay up shopping online and obsessively reading product reviews or emailing friends. I began embracing the need for healing and the process was underway when I soon learned that as great of a person my husband was, he was not equipped or willing to handle the diagnosis. This was a painful awakening because it was a time when I was struggling to find the right medications and addressing some painful issues in counseling. I wanted him to understand and give me what he just didn't have to offer.

My attempt at normalcy created an even greater gap in between the two of us. Adding to the challenges we faced was the financial hardship caused by the mania, and his overspending in an attempt to feel better about the downward spiral in our lives. My life partner was now in the grieving process because he had lost the infallible wife he envisioned me to be. I learned that men have a difficult time coping with things that they feel helpless over. He became extremely antagonistic toward me because he fell in love, as did many others, with the manic woman who appeared to be accomplishing it all. As I matured in counseling, I found the right combination of medications—slept more, lost weight, abandoned unhealthy relationships, and established accountability partners. Those who were willing to accept it and help in my healing would question me when they realized I had been up sending emails to them throughout the night. At times when my children noticed that I was staying up late, they would respectfully, gently and lovingly suggest that I get some rest. I thank God for them because they realize when that prompting is necessary and lovingly do so. It is done in a manner that makes me feel validated and cared for so I really appreciate it. In the relationship chapter, I will talk more about how it affected my marriage and the outcome.

Grieving the Loss of Good Health

"To everything there is a season, and a time to
every purpose under the heaven: ... A time to weep
and a time to laugh; a time to mourn..."
(Ecclesiastes 3:1-4 KJV)

As noted in the previous chapter, people are clearly suffering from Bipolar, Depression, Anxiety, and other Disorders, although not officially diagnosed. We are living in a society where people are not addressing mental health issues and, as a result, we are experiencing school shootings and public massacres. Guns are being targeted as the culprit, but my aim is to highlight the issues and problems in the individuals who pick up the gun and decide to go on a killing spree, commit crimes of passion or robberies to satisfy manic shopping episodes, etc...

Facing it often means experiencing the death of what you thought may have been a normal and controlled life. I would be remiss not to say "The life that you THOUGHT was normal and controlled," because control is an illusion. Dr. Dharius Daniels explains that we can fill out an application for a job or mortgage, but God is the one who controls whether it comes to pass or not. As with all deaths, there is the normal sequence of grief that has been defined by Elisabeth Kübler- Ross in her 1969 book *On Death and Dying*. It's the way we were wired, so it's perfectly fine to feel each and every emotion. Dr. Daniels also states that, we are responsible for managing our emotions by allowing them to ride in the passenger seat but not drive the vehicle that carries us through life.

Denial

Initially, there is the **denial** stage because you desperately want your life, the person who is ill, or if it is you, to be well. Although I did experience this, I was able to move through it pretty quickly because I had a great support system. I was also driven by the need to swiftly move from the constant crying spells that I was experiencing. My crying spells met me in the morning, during working hours between clients, and in the evenings when I was supposed to be parenting my children. My husband, on the other hand, simply refused to accept it and minimized the issue altogether. I recall giving him the download of Julie Fast's book called *Loving Someone with Bipolar* because the book had just been completed and she gave free versions in exchange for feedback. We read the book, but it did not prompt a shift in the way he interacted with me. However, people have always talked about denial as something negative, but denial can be a healthy reaction when you are initially faced with grief. "Whatever the mind cannot contain, it will impose on the body." (Pastor A. R. Bernard, Sr.) I believe that denial can be the buffer to protect you from becoming ill or devastated to the point of no return when you are faced with the vicissitudes of life. When I speak of the vicissitudes of life, I am referring to the difficult times that we all go through: sickness, job loss, and other unwelcomed episodes. Although denial holds a natural component that protects our emotional stability, it can become unhealthy if it is prolonged or left unchecked.

Anger

Then there are the feelings of frustration and embarrassment that leads to **anger** while in the fog because you have no control over what is taking place. Unfortunately, this is a period where a great deal of the damage is done from people lashing out. Saying things like "She's crazy," "He's crazy," "I'm crazy," "Why me?" I was angry because, while I appreciated the support from close friends, I desperately wanted the acceptance and support of my life partner. I was angry that I had to take medication and be faced with trying a myriad of treatments because of severe allergies and sensitivities to medication. I was angry because I had to follow a budget. I was angry because I had to sleep and could no longer live an undisciplined life. Although mania is dangerous, it can be quite appealing and challenging to step away from. I believe that because men are fixers, my husband felt frustrated and angry that this was something he just couldn't fix. I believe he was also angry because caring for me meant that the attention he wanted was sacrificed in the process. Again, none of this means that he's a bad person, but rather a person guided by unmet expectations and needs. However, I viewed him as an enemy from my sensitive mental state, and not an ally, that I had to defend myself against. Unfortunately, in this delicate state, a believer may have a difficult time wrapping their minds around the reality of Ephesians 6:10–18 which tells us that we wrestle not against flesh and blood but the schemes of Satan. This state of mind creates a problem with focusing on the real enemy, and debilitates your ability to carry out the necessary warfare against Satan's attacks.

Bargaining

Once past the anger, the **bargaining** begins because you wonder what you could have done differently to completely avoid this. We wonder if we had gotten medical attention or counseling sooner, been a better person, born from a different gene pool, or ate better, then this wouldn't have happened. I remember becoming sin conscious and was repeating the repentant process for anything I thought back to doing in my past. This was in hopes that God would recall the diagnosis and give me a fresh start. A paradigm shift in this instance realizes that all things are not good or from God, but that He, in His infinite wisdom and powerful ability, has already designed a plan for it to work out for our good.

Depression

This stage can manifest in various forms of isolation until you can grip the reality of what has happened. This was a difficult stage for me because it ultimately added to the depression that I was already experiencing as a result of the illness. It is a place that the fogginess is most prevalent because you feel like you have rocks on your shoulders. You can feel as if you are dragging your full weight around in a potato sack tossed over your shoulder. Years ago, there was a cartoon called Charlie Brown, and he had a teacher whose face they never showed. The words she and the other adults in the cartoon expressed would always come across as "wa wa wa wa," and I often say that this is what depression feels like. The lack of focus often makes you feel as if you are in a fog, and the words with your limited concentration sound like that whiny "wa wa wa wa" that Charlie Brown's teacher and adults spoke in the cartoon. It is a place that creates more anger and guilt because of your limited functionality. I felt a tremendous amount of guilt because, after all, I was a wife, mother, employee, and counselor who could not fulfill my responsibilities the way others around me were.

Acceptance

In this final stage, you are convinced that the situation is out of your control, and you can't turn back or change it. Once I arrived at this point, I was more than willing to face it head on, and do whatever I needed to do to get stable. It was at this point that I began to openly talk about it to people who I believed would be accepting of it and not judge me as a Christian who lacked faith or was claiming something I should not claim. Yes, we do believe that we are to call things as though they were when walking by faith. Doing so does not mean you deny the reality, because how would God get the Glory if we don't state what existed and was fixed by Him? This was when I gained firsthand experience about just how uncomfortable discussing mental illness to others was. I also experienced how it felt to be labeled, judged and rejected because of it.

Unfortunately, **"The Five Stages of Loss and Grief"** are not always sequential and often resurface many times over when you least expect them to. Take heart in the realization that these feelings are universal and don't make you a bad person. After all, what's more important than what has taken place, is your ability to have faith in

God and move through the fog to the victorious testimony that God has designed for you?

Why Not Meds?

"... that ye present your bodies a living sacrifice,
holy, acceptable unto God, which is your
reasonable service."
(Romans 12:1 KJV)

When someone has bipolar disorder, there is a great deal of care that is required, as with any other illness. I am not saying that some mental illnesses are not the work of demonic activity, because that exists as exemplified in the Bible. But every illness in the Bible was not healed by exorcism, which tells me that there are not only different roots, but there are various methods of healing to be considered. Bipolar disorder is an illness that is caused by a neurochemical imbalance in the brain. As with any other ailment or imbalance, medication is most often required. I am clear that psychotropic medications have a terrible stigma tied to them and the side effects can be unbearable. In spite of that, we are required to do all that we have to do to present our bodies, and the brain is a part of the body, as a living sacrifice that is acceptable unto God.

We wouldn't shun a person who has to take chemotherapy for cancer, insulin for diabetes, cholesterol medications for high cholesterol, get a cast for a fracture, or is addressing any other disease. Of course there are some people who believe solely in herbal or natural remedies, but they are still taking something. As previously stated, I had a terrible time finding medications that I could tolerate because I am extremely sensitive to both prescribed and herbal treatments. For some reason, people are more accepting of natural remedies or pills that are offered in the health food stores. I am not against that option, but God had to show me that if a physician prescribes medication based on your height, weight, age, the severity of your condition and other factors, then how could the recommended dosage on the bottle of a health food store product be a good fit all? However, if you have found something in that area to help you for any condition, that is wonderful.

We spend a great deal of the time judging and criticizing methods rather than embracing whatever way God has chosen to heal our individual ailments. The Bible shows us that many methods were used to bring about healing. There was the dipping seven times at a specific location, casting out demons, spit and mud mixed together, and many more, so why not medication? Everything is initially made by God and for God, but Satan corrupts and has taken the lives of many by dissuading them away from the things that can help them. Think about the many people who are in prison and could have benefited from proper treatment and how they may not have taken innocent lives if brought to mental stability with medical care.

Once I found the right medication, I was able to think clearer and see that some of my decisions were not in line with the principles of God's Word. I was able to sleep better, and that alone helped me to have a better perspective as well as manage other health issues. I had an easier time focusing enough to read God's Word for long periods of time and better hear God's still small voice (promptings). Managing the mood swings helped me better comply with God's Word in the areas of finance, relationships, and more. However, the balancing of this illness does not rest in a pill. That was just the beginning because it also enabled me to move through counseling from the fog to successfully obtaining the transformed mind that God commands us to have in Romans 12:2. I continue to believe God that one day His work on the cross for our healing will manifest to the point where medication is not required. Even if it doesn't happen down here, I know without a shadow of a doubt that it's not because God can't do it. It is an enemy, and He said that He would make our enemies our footstool, so I will use it as a footstool to step on and reach people in need, to minister, and to get to where God wants me to be in this life.

I recently received an online petition regarding this issue. We must help each other through first being honest about our circumstances and seeking help before things are out of control.

On New Year's Day of 2015, 21-year-old Mathew Ajibade, a student of Savannah Technical College in Georgia, was taken to the police station after a domestic disturbance call. When police responded to the call, Mathew's girlfriend told the police Mathew suffered from bipolar disorder, and that he was having a manic episode, and she gave the police his medication. The best response under such circumstances would have been to transport Ajibade to a medical facility. But they didn't. They took him to the police station.

During the booking process, Mathew became uncooperative, and deputies at the Chatham County

Detention Center responded with force, which included blows to his face and head. He was subsequently cuffed, hogtied, taken to an interrogation room, and strapped to a restraining chair and tased in the groin. Left unattended, Mathew died in the restraining chair.

In October 2015, in Chatham County Superior Court a jury acquitted the officers involved—Jason Kenny and Maxine Evans—of charges of involuntary manslaughter. The jury convicted Officer Jason Kenny of a lesser charge: cruelty to an inmate, a felony which carries a sentence of up to 3 years in jail. Judge James Bass took the liberty of his power and issued a 'creative' sentence of only one month in jail, and three months of probation instead. Kenny was also allowed to serve the jail time only on weekends, in the very jail where he once worked.

Father God, in the name of Jesus, I pray that whatever the diagnosis, the person in need will receive the understanding necessary to overcome every obstacle relative to their affliction. You said in Your Word that many are our afflictions, but You deliver us out of them ALL. I pray that they will be willing to follow the path that You have designed for the manifestation of their individual healing to protect themselves and those around them. I pray that people in authority will have a better understanding and training in handling people with mental health challenges in Jesus' name.

Therapy

"And be not conformed to this world: but be ye
transformed by the renewing of your mind, that ye
may prove what is that good, and acceptable, and
perfect, will of God."
(Romans 12:2 KJV)

Medication alone does not bring balance to a person with bipolar or any other disorder. There are things that you experience and handle that those closest to you cannot convey or hold you accountable for. Over the years, I have heard people say that they only wanted to see a Christian counselor for their issues. I have had such well trained and caring professionals that were from different belief systems that God has used to help me become stable. Do you ask your physician their denomination before receiving medical treatment from them?

By the time I had entered treatment at age 40, I had made so many life-altering decisions that spiraled my life into chaos. One of the worst environments for a person suffering from mental illness is a chaotic and disorganized environment. As long as I was manic and not sleeping, I was able to keep up with the housework and all the other things I delved into without counting the cost. Once I began sleeping, we had several conversations in couples counseling about how important it was for me to have the help I needed to live in a healthy and organized environment. This meant that the children would need to learn how to carry their weight as well as my spouse, but that did not happen.

My husband is the product of another culture, and his thinking was that the women should take care of the home while the children have fun at all times. I am sharing this only so that you can have a clear picture of how important it is to choose wisely the people you allow into your life when you suffer from mental illness. I am also highlighting the need for others to understand that it will take some sacrificing of your own ideas and desires if you choose to be in the life or have to work with someone who suffers from mental illness. We had a relationship that became toxic, and in order for me to get well, I had to disassociate myself. My daughter opted to live with her dad and, therefore, remained in the home. That does not mean that God can't change people or heal toxicity, but you have to want to be healed. In John 5:6, Jesus asked the man at the pool of Bethesda who was lame for thirty-eight years if he wanted to be healed. When the man said yes, he told him to take up his bed and walk. The truth is, it takes a joint effort with God at the center to make relationships work, and to be healed—but some people are not willing (an issue of the WILL) to do what it takes to reach that end.

Therapists are trained to quickly identify when a person is in a dangerous place, and they have an obligation to report when you are a danger to yourself, or to someone else. The existing chaotic environment did not foster the wisdom and restraint necessary for parenting a rebellious teenager. This was mostly because my husband deliberately sabotaged my directives to prove that he was the head of the house and not me, so that completely challenged my ability to parent in a healthy way. Although there were several other factors that led to this incident, the extremes that your emotions can evolve to with the disorder played a huge part in an almost consequential incident.

It was Monday morning when I attended my regular counseling session with my counselor. I was discussing the events of my weekend, and the issues I faced, as I generally did in the counseling sessions. My daughter had just turned fourteen, and we arrived at a heated discussion about something that I wanted her to do. Things happened so quickly that I don't recall all of the details that led to me punching her in the face. After the incident, like the many heated arguments that ended in me throwing things at my husband, we experienced the calm that was encompassed by a cloud of guilt after the storm. I remember telling my counselor what happened in a matter of fact way because it was just another series of the ongoing dramas in my path.

No sooner than I arrived home that afternoon, I received a telephone call from my therapist telling me that I had to return to the office the next day so that she could call The Division of Youth and Family Services to report the incident. When I arrived at her office, she apologized profusely for having to take this step. I assured her that although I had many feelings about it, the minute I heard her voice on the phone, I knew as a professional in the field of counseling that she was obligated to report. I sat present while she made the call, explained the incident, and detailed my ongoing treatment plan with her at that agency. She explained that I was extremely vigilant in my pursuit of emotional health and implementing loving parenting practices. She informed them that she did not see me as a continued imminent threat to myself or anyone. She explained that I was in a tumultuous marriage where our parenting styles were at opposite ends of the spectrum. She added that she believed it was my frustration and feeling that my calm attempts at parenting were being sabotaged by my husband's parenting style, which caused this incident to escalate.

They agreed to only chart it as a self-reporting incident provided that our entire family entered counseling. This outcome further confirmed my confidence in Romans 8:28 in that "...all things really do work together for those who love God and are the called according to His purpose." For so long, I could see that the illness was devastating my children, especially my daughter, but I did not know what to do about it. I was happy to see that she was placed in the hands of someone who may be able to help her sort things out and begin to heal. The therapeutic environment is designed to keep the person with mental illness safe and accountable for their actions. For people on the other end of this who are dealing with someone mentally ill, therapy can also provide the necessary support to guide you through the fog.

Lord Jesus, You said that in the multitude of counsel, there is safety. Keep Your people safe by not letting them rest until they submit to the therapeutic care needed to bring glory to You out of this affliction.

Mood Swings

"A double minded man is unstable
in all of his ways."
(James 1:8 KJV)

People with Bipolar Disorder experience mood swings. At times you are very stable, but at times I could actually feel my mood shift from depression to joyful, and back to depression or anger. Along with depression comes irritability, so at times I would be happily playing with my children, and suddenly there would be a shift in my mood. For a long time, I would hurt my children because I would become angry, and they couldn't understand why. This also happened a great deal when I was a teenager. My family and I would simply be enjoying each other's attention and joking around. At some point during our gathering, I would take something personal and end up in my room in tears, and sinking into depression.

My daughter, whose perception you will hear more about in a later chapter, bore the brunt of most of my anger and mood swings because I entered treatment when she was nine years old. Up until that time, I would spend a great deal of the day screaming at her. All of my efforts to behave differently were fruitless, but I continued to try. I once read a book by James Dobson called *Help for Screaming Parents*. The book had some great strategies and exposed the things that led up to the screaming. It helped to get us through this challenge, and every night, I would apologize at bedtime to her and tell her that it was not her fault that I was screaming. I often prayed that her self-esteem would not be damaged by this. We would pray together those nights for God to help me and for tomorrow to be a better day.

Although I continued to have these mood swings for years, prayer, medication, and treatment taught me how to handle them. I began to tell my children whenever my mood changed that I was feeling overstimulated. They would step back and give me the space that I needed for it to pass. As I began to learn more about the illness, I was able to teach them and the people around me about it, and I learned ways to make necessary adjustments when I wasn't feeling well. I am so grateful for the children that God gave me because although they have faced many challenges, they have done their best to be gracious and supportive.

Although I did not scream at people I worked with, the mood swings and irritability would lead to arguments or heated discussions. They contributed to problems in the marriage because as a companion, your spouse wants and deserves attention. My husband was not able to understand that the mood swings were part of the illness, so he interpreted them as me not wanting to be bothered and rejection. I also became very agitated and violently threw things at him during arguments. That doesn't mean that people with bipolar cannot have successful marriages. There were already some deep rooted issues in both of our personalities, thought processes, and past which impacted our marriage. After many years, I retrospectively realize that cultural differences affected our ability to see things from each other's perspective. By spending as much time in the Word as possible, following my treatment plan, my moods have become steadier than they have ever been before.

I cannot stress enough how important it is to spend as much time as possible reading the Word of God. The Bible is filled with stories of triumph over life's challenges. All that was written in the scriptures show you that God is with us through every challenge and that He is not looking for perfect people to use. The more time I spent in the Word, healing and stability became a reality to me. Nowadays, I spend a great deal of time laughing because the Bible says that a merry heart is like medicine. I confess regularly as I take communion at home that by God's stripes, I was healed. I believe that I am healed, although I continue to take medication and attend counseling, because that is what God says in His Word.

Dear Heavenly Father, I pray that You will help us to be stable in all of our ways. I pray that we will continue to be surrounded by joy and laughter so that the healing process and recovery can manifest. This I ask in The Matchless Name of Jesus. I thank You that there is joy and peace in The Holy Spirit that ministers to us in our darkest of times.

Decisions

"But don't begin until you count the cost. For who would begin construction of a building without first calculating the cost to see if there is enough money to finish it?"
(James 1:8 NLT)

Mental illness impacts a person's ability to make sound decisions and carry them out. I look back at the many whirlwinds that have been caused by my inability to make sound decisions and thank God that I am, first, still alive, and secondly, able to live a productive and stable life today. I will later discuss in more detail the impact mental illness has had on the way in which I approached education. At this juncture, I would like to use it as an example of how challenging my decision to return to school affected our lives.

I had been a Substance Abuse Counselor for nine years when I decided to return to school. Often it wasn't just the impulsive decisions that I made but the impulse and anxiety to get it done immediately that caused a negative outcome. Because my finances never gained a consistently favorable momentum, I became increasingly disturbed by my inability to rise above a certain salary. My degree in Theology had opened the door to counseling, but when I wanted to see an increase in my salary and began looking, I learned that the jobs I was interested in required different types of degrees. A great deal of the requirements that are thrust on applicants has to do with the saturation of applications submitted daily to human resources departments via the internet. I have seen God open doors that you are not quite qualified for, like when I transitioned from banking to counseling, but you have to get the education needed to sustain it once you are through that door. I did exactly that by completing coursework in HIV/AIDS, substance abuse and Mentally Ill and Chemically Dependent areas.

So, in my frustration with financial stagnation, I made a decision that ultimately made things worse instead of better. I not only decided to return to school full-time, but I also selected a major of study that required extra work and a study abroad experience. My husband was very supportive, since I highlighted that this decision would eventually get us out of the financial hole we were in. However, we did not know about the sacrifices we would be forced to make when we were signed up. My daughter was nine, and my son was six, so they still needed quite a bit of attention. Many people are able to go to school, raise children, take care of a home, and more, but when you add something else to an already full plate, something will fall off. When you add more to a plate that has the crack of mental or any other illness in it, you already have things seeping through the cracks and now you have things falling off as well. Sound decisions require a close observation and consideration of what is falling off and seeping through the cracks of your plate.

My husband was working, so he was only able to do the bare minimum at home, as overtime was necessary to sustain us. This led to more tension in the household because of intense arguments when he wanted attention at times when I had to study. I wasn't bringing in a salary, was living off student loans and getting further and further away from the financial freedom I was seeking. School was stressful, and it did a number on our already strained marriage. This also spiraled down to the children because now they were living in a true war zone. Thank God for His mercy and supplying all of our basic needs because, again, we were faithful tithers.

This decision was just followed by other bad ones also because when manic, which I happened to experience more than being depressed, you are anxious and want everything to happen fast. You engage in behaviors clearly foolish, just not seen by you as such. Although an immersion experience is a necessary element in acquiring another language, the way I went about it wasn't the best approach. With the anxiety, I wanted to see the language acquisition happen yesterday. However, with the mania, I couldn't sit down and settle into my books or focus for the learning process to happen in order to gain the needed foundation.

My first trip was to Madrid, Spain and that was a five-week trip in the summer. I was still on the hundred level coursework, so with the language learning process being slower after age thirteen, I had not learned enough or studied enough for that trip to be beneficial. It was very stressful, and added to that experience was my children being in Florida with my parents.

They volunteered to go, and I was so happy because my parents retired to Florida before I settled down to have children. I saw this as an opportunity for them to get to know my parents. My children ended up in a living hell because a family member living near my parents did not approve of them being there. Added to that stress were my wonderful traditional classmates who wanted very little to do with me because I reminded them of the parent they didn't want watching over their shoulders. This was an opportunity of a lifetime when they were clear across the country finally exposed to freedom, so my presence cramped their style. My parents were elderly and so overwhelmed by the intense pressure from the other family member that they did not know how to defuse it. As a result, the occasion that was for them to connect with their grandparents turned into my children just staying out of sight in the room and watching television most of the time. When I returned to retrieve my children, they looked like orphans, and that sent me into a downward spiral.

Father, help us to make decisions that are in line with the plans and purposes that You have for our lives. Let our decisions count as bringing glory to You and adding to Your Kingdom. I pray for all those who have been negatively affected by the decisions of those who are mentally ill. I am asking You to heal their wounds and make the broken places straight in Jesus' name.

Jélissa's Story

"... 'From the lips of children and infants you,
Lord, have called forth your praise?"
(Mathew 21:16 NIV)

As previously stated, my daughter bore the brunt of most of my illness because I was not diagnosed or treated until she was nine. We have open discussions about the ways in which this has affected my children, and because of those discussions, I am able to share her heart. Initially, I had no idea how to convey the diagnosis to my daughter. My best attempt led to me purchasing a book by Bebe Moore Campbell (Author), and E. B. Lewis (Illustrator) called *Sometimes My Mommy Gets Angry*. The book reminds the little girl to call her grandmother when her mother is very sad and angry, and her grandma would reassure her that her mother loves her. It was one of the very few books available for children with parents suffering from mental illness. There have since been other contributions to that end. Angela Holloway has written a wonderful book specific to bipolar disorder called *The Bipolar Bear Family: When a Parent Has Bipolar Disorder*.

One of the greatest challenges for her was seeing how extremely angry I became toward my husband. They would hear the arguing, but I was the one throwing things and screaming, so when it came time to separate, she remained with her father, and my son moved out with me. Because she saw my behavior and experienced it firsthand, the separation was, from her perspective, entirely my fault. After a year of me living on my own in a nontoxic environment, she began to see the manageability of the illness and the kind characteristics that had always been present outside of the illness and relationship. In a recent conversation with a friend whose mother had paranoid schizophrenia, she shared that after her father passed away, her mother's illness became totally manageable.

Jélissa was most affected by mental illness when they stayed with my parents while I was in Madrid, Spain for five weeks. Although this was a voluntary visit that they looked forward to, as previously mentioned, it quickly turned sour. The family member that disapproved of them being there also exhibited signs of mental illness beginning in her youth.

There was the constant fighting in school, promiscuity, disappearing for weeks at a time, and stealing money from her parents. She eventually became pregnant at sixteen and left school. Her rage and mood swings have always been extreme, which eventually drove a wedge between her and her children. Her children were able to resolve their hurt when they came to the realization that she exhibited traits of bipolar disorder and encouraged her to get treatment. She would not seek help, so they were afraid of her rages and saddened that it prevented them from having a healthy relationship with the loving and caring mother they knew existed within.

There were times during those five weeks that my children were there that she had moments where she attempted to be nice to Jélissa. Once she was given a life-sized doll by her employer and decided to give it to Jélissa. I guess her mood shifted on her way to my parent's house because she ended up throwing the doll at my daughter when she arrived at the house.

As previously stated, my mother was under a tremendous amount of pressure because there was also another issue going on at the time, and my father was arguing with her daily about it. She became so stressed that she was unkind to Jélissa as well. My mother couldn't see through her own fog to offer the love and compassion of a grandmother, since their father nor I was in a position to rescue her from this family member's attacks.

Father God, in the Name of Jesus, there are children all over this world who have and are still suffering from the effects of their parent's challenges with mental illness. Father, I ask that You help and heal them. Please allow nothing that has transpired in the relationship between them and their parents to be used by the devil to destroy their destiny. I pray that they will see it for the illness that it is and not take it on personally as something that they have done wrong.

Oscar's Story

"God heard the boy crying, and the angel of God
called to Hagar from heaven and said to her,
"What is the matter, Hagar? Do not be afraid;
God has heard the boy crying as he lies there."
(Genesis 21:17 NIV)

The next decision I made to study abroad was in 2007, and I went for three months to San José, Costa Rica. Initially, my intention was to be there for a year with a break during the Christmas holiday. My daughter was just turning thirteen the month I left, and my son was nine years old. We were attending New York Christian Cultural Center in Brooklyn at the time, and leading up to the trip, our pastors A. R and Karen Bernard met with us and prayed with us on several occasions. They asked at every meeting whether my husband was sure that this was something he could handle, and he assured them that it was. I was convinced that this was the only way to have my language soar to the level that I was aiming for. Others questioned the wisdom in this decision, but there was no turning back for me.

While in Costa Rica, I had a wonderful Columbian counselor with whom I had weekly sessions by phone. She was also a Christian, so I was able to talk about different aspects of my faith. I lived with a widow in Tibás and will later discuss the use of wisdom when disclosing your mental health status to others. The country was amazing, and for the most part, it was a wonderful experience. My son, however, was struggling and felt abandoned.

My husband was not a strong disciplinarian nor had the level of energy that it takes to manage a home while caring for young children and maintaining a full-time job. Thereby, the house was disorganized and in shambles, and their nutrition was sorely lacking. My son has ADHD and spent a year in anger management therapy because he often went from zero to one hundred in crisis situations. I would monitor his progress in school because of it and made sure that the supports set in place through his 504 Plan, which was a less stringent Individual Education Plan, were still meeting his needs. My children were clear that although we were living in a climate where children are disrespecting teachers and causing all sorts of distractions in class, this behavior would not be tolerated by me.

My son had become disruptive and began to decline in his school work. He started acting out in front of his teacher, and at the same time, the environment I was in began to weigh so heavily on me that I had to leave a few weeks early. Although I was exercising daily and lost twenty pounds, I was still in a deep depression—largely in part because I was experiencing the same, if not, worse rejection from my classmates as I did in Spain. A huge part of it was my being a parental reminder, but another part of it on both occasions was religious persecution. My counselor concurred and wrote a letter of support for me to finish my finals early so that I could return home. Being Hispanic, she understood the nuances of the culture and their lack of sensitivity to my illness.

When I visited Oscar's school, his teacher told me how he had become really sad, and that sadness eventually turned to anger. A friend helped me trick my husband into picking me up at the airport by saying she needed him to get a friend for her. I was unrecognizable at first because of the 20 pounds I had lost. That was easy because the host family was required to cook and clean the house, which afforded me time to exercise daily and eat healthy meals. My children came downstairs at 2:00 A.M. wiping the sleep out of their eyes, and my son ran to hold me really tight. I recall taking him to school the following day and realizing again that all things really do work together for our good. God is truly in control even when we take a wrong turn. He allowed the heat to be turned up, forcing me to come home, and his teacher confirmed that she didn't think he could have lasted another day without me.

My son explained that his decline started when there was a parent teacher's night that his father forgot to attend. The following day, when the teacher commented about all of the parents she had the pleasure of meeting, he felt embarrassed, abandoned and uncared for. This was a clear example of how anger is a secondary emotion that manifests when the initial feelings go unexpressed and unresolved. Anger generally begins as frustration, embarrassment, rejection and other emotions that go unresolved and eventually turns to anger. He said that he also knew that he would not be held accountable for acting out because of his father's relaxed parenting style. I remember walking down the street with him, and for weeks, he would hold my hand, and the force that he squeezed it with reminded me how much he missed me, and how important my presence is in his life. Thank God that through a series of financial issues, I was relieved of my commitment to return to Costa Rica for another semester as previously intended. Oscar still speaks openly about that season of his life, but I thank God for healing, and I thank

God for my son's forgiveness as well.

Father, I thank You that even when we fall short as parents, You are a father to the fatherless and a mother to the motherless. I thank You that You love our children and have plans to prosper them in spite of our illness. I pray that You continue to heal any brokenness and erase any traces of their wounds in Jesus' name.

Money and Bipolar

"The plans of the diligent lead surely to abundance,
but everyone who is hasty comes only to poverty."
(Proverbs 21:5 ESV)

Bipolar and other disorders significantly affect a person's ability to make sound financial decisions as well as resist the temptation of impulsive spending. With finances being one of the top ten reasons that marriages fail, it presents a different level of challenges to manage the illness. The added stress of finances and the marital strain further exacerbates the illness. There were times, until God leveled me off and taught me how to manage the illness, when I would feel a burning desire and anxiety to go on an uncontrollable shopping trip. Most often, this was a decorating idea, and when this happens, you fail to count the cost. The best way for me to combat these things was to deal solely with cash and not cards. I was more than willing to freeze my bank card because it would give me time to count the cost; however, my husband was unwilling to leave his in the freezer for fear of an emergency going unaddressed. You might say or wonder what that had to do with me freezing my cards, but when we were together, I could convince him to use his for what I wanted because spending made him feel better also. I cringe when thinking of the money lost on overdraft fees paid out because I was, at times, spending money on bank cards that was not there.

Besides attempting to use cash more frequently, which gives a clear vision of what you have, I utilize an application on my smartphone called *You Need A Budget* that allows me to journal my expenses as I go along. It keeps me clear on what I have and helps with my desire not to spend every penny that I have. I also decline overdraft protection so that if I exceed what I have, the purchase will be rejected. I thank God because I can actually see His hand of prevention when I am about to make an unwise purchase. I believe that there are things ahead that God can see that we can't, and if you do all that you can to be a good steward, God will do the rest. God said that He would rebuke the devour for our sake, if we bring our tithes and offering to the storehouse. Oftentimes I was to be rebuked from devouring my own crops. Praise God for his faithfulness and shutting the door on some of my attempts to make a wrong move.

There is so much in God's word about money and how to handle it, and people, at times, judge a person's indiscretions as disobedience or foolishness without understanding what the root of it is. The one thing that I was consistent with, because of my conviction to put God first, was tithing. *"Will a man rob God? Yet you rob me. "But you ask, How do we rob you? In tithes and offerings ... Bring the whole tithe into the storehouse, that there may be food in my house. Test me in this," says the LORD Almighty, "and see if I will not throw open the floodgates of heaven and pour out so much blessing that you will not have room enough for it"* (Malachi 3:8, 10 NIV). I believe that had I not been faithful with my tithing, we would have suffered greater harms like eviction, bankruptcy, or more because of this illness. Returning to God what belongs to him in tithes and offerings promises a hedge of protection that if absent, we could otherwise be consumed.

God, I thank You that You were gracious enough to allow only the things to befall me in the area of finances that were designed to teach and draw me nearer to You. Thank You that although I experienced some alarming situations, You continued to be faithful at honoring Your Word and not allowing me to be consumed. I pray that You will continue to use me to show others that in spite of this ailment, they can still successfully and consistently manage finances through You in Jesus' name.

Relationships and Bipolar

"An offended friend is harder to win back than a fortified city. Arguments separate friends like a gate locked with bars."
(Proverbs 18:19 DBT)

If it is possible, as far as it depends on you, live at peace with everyone.
(Romans 12:18 NIV)

I've shared throughout this writing how mental illness affected my relationships within my family. I'd like to further explain the issues surrounding this illness that causes devastation to relationships unless the people involved understand it and possess God's unconditional agape love in their hearts. However, even if those factors exist, we all have limitations.

First, there is the pressure to speak that exists with bipolar disorder. The Bible speaks against idle chatter and how sin commonly begins to take place in the form of gossip, judgment, self-exhortation and quarreling; so, for these reasons, offenses are inevitable. Once a person is offended, you cannot take your words back, and as Proverbs 18:19 KJV states, **"A brother offended is harder to be won than a strong city: and their contentions are like the bars of a castle."**

I have lost some wonderful relationships in these cases, but with this and other frailties, I still believe that God can use it for our good because He is a God who wastes nothing. Even if it is a lesson on how to interact with others while demonstrating the love of Christ, I believe God takes our mess and makes a message out of it.

Regulating emotions are a part of the illness, so I've spent a great deal of time, whether feeling awfully angry or extremely happy, going on and on about situations. It is usually at that point that I would begin passing judgment and offending the listener. I often think back remembering that from the onset of this illness, my mother would have a difficult time calming me down once I became upset. God has moved me through a season of quietness where I've spent hours in the Word, and it has blessed me with more self-control so that I do not fall into idle chatter. Another strategy that God has taught me is to consistently take in the Word and other information so that when I am feeling the pressure to speak, I can impart wisdom and be a blessing with what I am saying. My gift of gab is exactly that, a gift, but our gifts can also be a curse if unchecked or if there is another issue (such as the case with bipolar disorder) that leads to the enemy using it for evil.

God, I pray that you will help us to tame our tongues so that we can be a blessing to those around us. I thank You that in spite of lost relationships, You have blessed me with whoever I need to be in a relationship with. I thank You that You will always give us fruitful relationships to do life with and to bear each other's burdens in prayer.

Employment and Mental Illness

"Whatever you do, work at it with all your heart,
as working for the Lord, not for human masters,"
(Colossians 3:23)

Work life and your performance can be greatly affected when in the throes of mental illness. It is also one of the most stressful environments to be in because we spend more time at work than we do at home. In the work place we are forced to work with people that we do not select, and at times there issues can contribute to making the environment toxic for you. Most often, because of the illness, it is difficult to carry your weight at work. Sometimes this is due to a focus issue. My son's physician has explained that you can have Attention Deficit Hyperactive Disorder or Attention Deficit Disorder and not have Bipolar Disorder, but more often than not, you will have ADHD/ADD when you have Bipolar Disorder. If that is the case, it would be diagnosed as Comorbid Bipolar Disorder and can be difficult to treat. There is also a fine line between the two presenting difficulty with diagnosis in children and teenagers. At times, sitting at a desk or in meetings for long periods of time can be a challenge. Other times, when depression sets in, it affects attendance; however, mania can have the same impact because if you are not sleeping well, you will be distracted or unable to grasp simple concepts needed to perform your job. The inability to regulate emotions and process information rationally can lead to quarrels and strife on the job.

I worked in banking for thirteen years, and I remember struggling with attendance. During that time, I was having problems with a stomach ailment, hyperthyroidism and severe allergies. I was frequenting the doctor, but I was often on probation for taking time off work. Although the other ailments were legitimate and warranted time away from work, I would also become depressed whenever I had to be out, and that would extend the number of days away from work.

Co-workers and managers who don't know or understand what is going on can begin to become angry and frustrated because they feel saddled with that person's responsibilities. This can lead to unemployment, and thereafter, a downward spiral in other areas. Fortunately, in this day and age, we have the Family And Medical Leave Act (FMLA) which protects your job once your doctor has documented the illness with your employer. The best thing to do is to take good care of yourself because while your job is protected, they are not required to pay you if you don't have time available. If the absence goes beyond a few weeks, you may be able to collect short-term disability. Sometimes this adds more stress because people don't generally get the money from disability to pay their bills until they are back at work. It is also important to take care of yourself and do all that you can to fulfill your commitment to the job as if you are working unto the Lord. God does for us what we cannot do for ourselves, but we have a responsibility to participate in our recovery.

After leaving Wall Street when I became pregnant with my

daughter, I had a difficult time staying on a job more than a year. At times, the change was necessary because of downsizing or promotion, but my impulse for change would prompt the shift. There was a point where I stayed on a job for three years until I left to have my son. It was not a small agency, so there were several departments. The running joke was that I had only remained in each position for 6 months, but had worked in just about every department there was.

All of this is something that I became aware of while in counseling, but I give God glory for teaching me to check with and rest in Him before shifting. I thank God for the closed doors that He did not allow me to push past. That doesn't mean that I am perfect in all of my actions, but praise God that He knows how to find us and get us back on track. God is the GPS of our lives if you allow Him to be, and like the GPS, He will recalculate the route to get us where we need to be regardless of the road we are on. I will discuss ways to avoid this in the final chapter on taking care of yourself or the person in your life with mental illness.

Lord, help those with mental illness and the people that they work with understand the impact and extend grace. Lord, help those who suffer from mental illness get the help that they need to thrive in the workplace. Let them not expect their place of employment to extend grace while they sit idle and not seek mental health care for themselves.

Education and Mental Illness

... let the wise listen and add to their learning, and let the discerning get guidance for understanding proverbs and parables, the sayings and riddles of the wise. The fear of the Lord is the beginning of knowledge, but fools despise wisdom and instruction.
—Proverbs 1:5–7 NIV

Even people with mental illness have gifts and callings. God does not revoke the gifts or callings that He has given to us because of illness. Of course if we don't learn to manage any illness, we will not experience the fullness of our destiny. We have an obligation to get the training and education necessary to fine tune our gifts, talents, and abilities as well as obtain whatever credentials necessary to utilize them.

I not only have bipolar disorder, but I also have ADHD, so focusing for the length of time to study on a college level can be a challenge. I struggled for a long time until one day, through one of my jobs, I was introduced to The Division of Vocational Rehabilitation. This is an agency that assists people with mental illness, addictions and other disabilities to gain employment or training that leads to employment. Their services are quite expansive, and they are extremely supportive.

It was a challenge getting them to approve financial support for my degree work because college is very stressful and can cause a person with mental illness to spiral. Their concern was that they would invest money in something that I would not be unable to complete. God gave me favor, and they agreed to assist me financially, and my counselor was phenomenal and provided a great deal of emotional support. They did, however require me to meet with my therapist regularly.

The other thing I was introduced to was the Office of Disabilities in college. This department provides all college students with the support they need for their specific disability. You are required to bring documentation of your disability, and it is evaluated to determine the type of accommodations that will be extended to you. In my case, I was given time and a half for test taking, and extensions on assignments when necessary. You would be given a sealed letter from that office with your professor's name on it, and it would outline accommodations in which they should extend to you. At that time you discuss your accommodation with the professor, it was you decision to disclose or not to disclose your disability. You and the professor would then discuss ways in which to communicate during times when you might need allowances.

At that time, school was extremely stressful because of the difficult major I had selected, and because of the many relational challenges and demands at home. It was necessary for me to take full advantage of these accommodations because I was often in and out of depression and spiraling into mania. Although extremely stressful, I continued pressing forward until my mother became ill, and it was necessary for me to travel back and forth to Florida on a regular basis. Initially, I made every effort by carrying my computer back and forth to continue my studies, but I was often sleeping in the hospital at night and keeping my father occupied during the day, so I eventually had to withdraw. My relationship with DVR ended prior to that because I became depressed when realizing that I could not continue with the Spanish major, as the commitment was not something I could handle.

Because there is so much awareness and support available, I would encourage anyone to first pray about attending school. If you believe it is God's timing, then you can handle it! To those in the life of someone with mental illness who wants to attend school, I encourage you to realize that it is unrealistic and unfair to expect them to serve you at the same level as before. Be kind to that person and kind to yourself by managing your expectations. Disappointment comes not from what we find but from what we expect to find.

God, I pray for all of those in school with challenges that threaten to impede their progress toward their calling. I believe that although it may take longer than others, that You will help us to do all that You have called us to. I thank You for the wisdom to know when to enter the arena of academia and for providing the support to get through it in Jesus' name.

Depression

"Peace I leave with you; my peace I give you. I do not give to you as the world gives. Do not let your hearts be troubled and do not be afraid."
(John 14:27 NIV)

This is not the depression that is related to the clinical component of the mental illness. This is the depression that even the disciples experienced when they realized that Jesus was going to the cross and would no longer be with them. The prophets of the Old Testament experienced depression, but these issues were situational and not clinical. Part of caring for your mental health includes getting to the root of these things and rehearsing what Jesus gave the disciples, in His Word.

"In my distress I called to the LORD; I called out to my God. From his temple he heard my voice; my cry came to his ears…"
(2 Samuel 22:7 NIV)

"The LORD is close to the brokenhearted and saves those who are crushed in spirit"
(Psalms 34:18 NIV).

*"A merry heart doeth good like a medicine: but a
broken spirit drieth the bones"
(Proverbs 17:22 KJV).*

*"The people walking in darkness have seen a great
light; on those living in the land of deep darkness
a light has dawned"
(Isaiah 9:2 NIV).*

*"But God, who comforts the depressed, comforted
us by the coming of Titus"
(2 Corinthians 7:6 NASB).*

Low self-esteem can also be the root of depression. In order to have healthy interactions, we must first love ourselves. The Bible says in Psalms 8:5 and Psalms 139:14 that we are children of God, uniquely original, made just a little lower than angels, fearfully and wonderfully made by God, in route to heaven, and winners.

Falling into the comparison trap leads to depression. We begin to look at what others have in comparison to us. Sometimes we feel better briefly because what we have is better than what someone else has, but that is temporarily soothing until someone else with something better comes along. This can be a comparison of our appearance, home, car, job, relationships, church, and gifts.

Lack of influence at home, workplace, school, or church can also lead to depression. You can speak to this by knowing that God will hear from you and allow you to move mountains through your prayers. Now that's influence, and you do matter!

God has also given you authority over sickness and decease, and that includes mental illness. It doesn't have to have control or authority over your life. Call upon the Lord night and day, and He will come to your aid. There are times when I have had a really stressful day, and every conversation was hard. Remember that I mentioned earlier that bipolar can make you behave combatively, so this would leave me feeling like I had just fought a losing battle. When I know that I am in a bad place, I say to God, "I am not feeling well." He knows that I am referring to the effects of the bipolar disorder, and shortly thereafter, I am feeling better. Sometimes it is on my pillow at night after evaluating the day, and His new mercy will meet me in the morning. This is an act of faith that God is answering my prayer to heal me of this illness as I claim my healing and do my part in the meantime. The more we acknowledge our need to be healed and the place that we are in, the more we walk in the process and experience the benefits of the stripes that Jesus obtained on the cross for our healing. You can experience the benefits of those stripes also.

God, please help those who, at times, have difficulty moving from their bed of depression (affliction) to pick up their bed and walk. In Jesus' name.

Wisdom in Disclosure

*"A gossip betrays a confidence, but a trustworthy
person keeps a secret."
(Proverbs 11:13 NIV)*

The truth about mental illness is not something that everyone is mature enough to handle. You must spend a significant amount of time with a person and listen to the way they handle confidences extended to them by others before you disclose your condition to them. You should also observe how they handle relational crisis. I recall a time when someone, who was supposed to be a friend, used my illness as a weapon to hurt me when I asked her to respect certain boundaries. Once she became angry, she stated that I must have forgotten to take my medication. I forgave it, but I was really hurt and shocked by her willingness, after being friends for so many years, to say anything to get what she wanted from me. As with addiction, sometimes the people around you want you to get better but don't want to give up the control they have over your life when you aren't stable.

Out of the abundance of the heart, the mouth speaks, so a person's views, perspectives, and attitudes toward mental illness will be exposed if you listen long enough. In deciding to disclose, unless you are called to give that person another perspective that can only be obtained through your personal testimony, then you may want to refrain from disclosing.

When I was initially diagnosed, I thought I could share that information with everyone, but I quickly found out that (for various reasons) it wasn't for everyone to know. One of the times that I most regretted sharing my condition was when I studied abroad in Costa Rica. I thought it important to do so because I was so far away from home.

Just as our culture is limited in our understanding of mental illness, so is that culture. I lived with a wonderful widow who took great care of me, but I was depressed most often and feeling isolated because I had no classmates my age, and I missed my family terribly. This woman was wonderful, but every behavior that she and others could not understand became a bipolar thing. This kind of judgment toward me exacerbated all that I was facing, and it added extra stress to my life. She often mentioned it in an effort to help me work through the depression, but it only added to my feeling misunderstood, alienated and ostracized. Although I was clear that it was not malicious, it did not stop me from feeling the way I did about it.

Over time, I have learned how to discuss my challenges with others. I have learned how to set limitations and boundaries without disclosing my illness. You, too, can learn how to have a conversation about your limitations without disclosure. If, for any reason, you disclose to someone whose maturity you misjudge and it yields an undesirable result, you can recover. Sometimes God will step in and completely remove that person from your life or He will give you the grace to endure. You have to have a forgiving heart through the power of Jesus within you. Unforgiveness will bring on stress that will, in turn, harm you and not the person who injured you. God promises in His Word that "you will be safe from slander and have no fear when destruction comes." (*Job 5:21 NIV*)

Father, You said that no man is an island and that we are to bear each other's burdens. You also said that if we have not wisdom, just ask it of You. I pray that You will continue to give us wisdom in the area of disclosure knowing that some experiences are not always for public but rather for private ministry (to those who are mature enough to handle it). Help us to embrace those You have blessed with the ability to walk alongside us. Be our Banner and rush in to help us if we have disclosed to wrong individuals who have used this illness as a weapon against us. Help us to overcome moments of fear, shame, embarrassment, and sadness when faced with such situations, in Jesus' name.

Chris Biehn's Story

(Self-Documented)

"It was good for me to be afflicted so that I might
learn your decrees."
(Psalm 119:71)

Before I had a relationship with Jesus, I felt lost, alone, and hopeless. There didn't seem to be a purpose for my life. I had a big ego and was worried about people pleasing. I would sin too often, and even though it felt wrong, I tried to disregard those feelings and rationalize these temptations. I grew up in the church, attended Sunday school, and completed confirmation. I had faith throughout my childhood, but after I got confirmed, I stopped going to church as regularly. I had a serious head injury at the end of 8th grade which my doctors today think triggered the dormant gene for Bipolar Disorder I. Throughout high school, I had a lot of challenges with mania and depression, and during my senior year, I became suicidal and depressed every other week. I was so angry at the world and doubted that God even existed. I was on the verge of becoming an atheist. When I was hospitalized at Johns Hopkins Psychiatric Ward, I was ranting to my fellow patients that I no longer believed in God. One of the patients handed me this book, *AHA: The God Moment That Changes Everything*, and insisted that I read it.

By the grace of God, I was able to read the book even in such a bad mental state and had my own 'aha' moment. It was then that I recognized that God was real (something that I really knew all along) and that I just didn't understand Him. I wanted to dedicate my life to understanding Him. I had to take the first semester off from Ithaca College due to health reasons. I then reconnected with my old pastor, and a friend introduced me to her Dad (Mr. Bazigian) who became my faith mentor. I went to Alpha at Fellowship Alliance Church, read several great books, and reaccepted Jesus as my personal savior. Re-finding Jesus was the most rewarding experience of my life! I regained hope, which is one of the most transformative things. I experienced so much joy and peace.

God has changed my life in remarkable ways. Since I have accepted Jesus as my personal savior, I have become more patient, slower to anger, more focused on helping others, more mindful of obeying the Bible and learning the Word. I am more forgiving, more eager for worship and prayer, more hopeful for eternity, and now I realize that everything in this life is temporary. Because of Christ, I want to share my faith with others, and I am slowly trying to eliminate envy, pride, and pleasing people. I am at a point where in times of trial, instead of asking "why me?" I try to ask, "Lord, what do you want me to learn from this?" My mantra is "it's not about me." I feel the Holy Spirit's work through me, and I no longer feel alone. I ask myself, *How can I love others today?* I believe the purpose for my pain is to help others who suffer in similar ways, and I plan to be a mental health advocate. I got a tattoo on my left wrist of a cross because I look at the cross as the ultimate sign of hope and healing. I look at the cross daily, and it is especially helpful when I'm depressed, so I can reframe my thoughts. Also, when I was suicidal, I had these evil thoughts (which I believe were from spiritual warfare) of slitting my wrist, so I have the cross as a permanent reminder not to act on these self-harming urges.

Since filming my YouTube video two years ago, I have continued experiencing intense bouts of depression. **Recently, I have learned to view my illness as one of the best things that has ever happened to me (which is a dramatically different perspective than I've had in the past) because I believe it's God's purpose for my life to help others who suffer in similar ways and to become a mental health advocate.** I also feel like my suffering has allowed me to become a more compassionate, empathetic, and genuine person.

Suicide

"Elijah was afraid[a] and ran for his life. When he came to Beersheba in Judah, he left his servant there ... He came to a broom bush, sat down under it and prayed that he might die. "I have had enough, Lord," he said. "Take my life; I am no better than my ancestors." Then he lay down under the bush and fell asleep. All at once an angel touched him and said, "Get up and eat." He looked around, and there by his head was some bread baked over hot coals, and a jar of water. He ate and drank and then lay down again."
(I Kings 19:3-6 NIV)

More often than not with mental illness and the impact it has on your life, there will come a point when you have a desire to end it all. As previously discussed, everyone gets depressed at some point. It's interesting to observe how people become depressed over some things while another person facing the same set of circumstances is able to cope and rise above what could easily get them down. It's also interesting to see how being depressed and discouraged distorts one's view of reality. This was even exemplified in the Bible when Elijah became discouraged and asked God to take his life. Judas made a successful attempt at suicide after he realized the impact of his decision to betray Jesus.

Suicide is simply a permanent solution to a temporary problem.

If you think back to many of the problems you have had, some of them are just a fleeting memory, and you survived. If the problem had a seriously negative affect on you, you will eventually be able to encourage others when you have persevered through it. Yes, some trials last longer than others, but God promises that He will deliver us out of every one of our afflictions. Nothing lasts forever, and if we keep the faith, a favorable outcome will manifest.

Unfortunately, the successful and attempted suicide rates are statistically larger than we would like to believe, but it happens. There are more than 2,000 suicides per day worldwide, leaving behind the bewildered and broken-hearted family and friends of that person. We also need to acknowledge that the number is far from accurate because there are cultures who cover it up because of their shame. Some attempts are never reported because of fear that they might be excluded from insurance or employment opportunities. Whether it be an attempt or complete suicide, it can leave others feeling as if they are in a fog. Death isn't something you truly recover from, but you can learn to reconcile your loss. As with the accounting principle of reconciliation, you will have your liability and asset columns. You will, thereafter, have to create a new normal. Survivors are left feeling blamed, judged and guilty by unintentionally harmful comments of others or their own thoughts.

In the first few days of their grief, they feel shocked and make statements such as, "This seems like a bad dream or a nightmare that I will never wake up from." "Can we just go back to yesterday when everything was normal?" or "I feel like I am in a fog and will never see my way clear again."

As time goes by, you may feel yourself moving into a deep depression which manifests into feelings of dejection, confusion, and/or anger. You may feel fatigued and unable to function enough to carry out your daily responsibilities. You may even, at times, enter into your own thoughts of committing suicide to avoid dealing with the pain of your tragic loss. Some people feel like they will never laugh again and cannot imagine life without their loved one.

It takes time to recover, depending on many factors such as the closeness of your relationship with that person, the manner in which they died, how widely publicized their death was, and other circumstances. No one can ever tell how long it will take an individual to reconcile their loss. Take, for example, a sibling that loses another sibling; if you've known this sibling all of your life, so whenever you make goals and life decisions that are without them, it is a constant reminder of the lost. When it is a parent, the parent is in no less pain but has spent years planning and setting goals prior to that child's birth. You will see in Angie's story how siblings are significantly impacted by the act of suicide.

Father, in the name of Jesus, I pray against the spirit of suicide. I pray Jeremiah 29:11 be infused in the minds and hearts of those who believe that they have no hope. I pray that they will see You in the midst of their struggles and not consider suicide as an option.

Angie's Story

"...What are relatives for if not to share trouble?"
(Proverbs 17:17 GNT

"...weeping may stay for the night, but rejoicing
comes in the morning."
(Psalms 30:5 NIV)

As mentioned in the dedication area, Angie's sister Nicole lost her battle with mental illness to suicide. She was not a believer in medication or therapy, and in spite of their attempts to talk her off the ledge, she eventually took her life a month after graduation and the week following her 18th birthday.

She was headed to college in New York City while Angie and her mom were planning to move closer to their mom's job. Angie had been bullied in her previous school and was looking forward to a fresh start. Her sister's mental illness had taken a toll on her since she was always the target of Nicole's rage. She was relieved that Nicole had made it through school and would be attending college. In spite of the chaos caused by the mental illness, she loved her sister dearly and was looking forward to a season where she would be more stable and they would have a better relationship. The Word says that unfulfilled hope makes the heart sick, so Angie was extremely disappointed that the amiable relationship she hoped for would never happen.

Nicole's suicide attempt took place in their home, but she was revived after her heart failed several times at the hospital. She was on life support for several days until the process of declaring her brain dead was completed. Her organs were donated, so the hospital stay was extended a bit further. During this time, all of her friends and family sat vigil at her bedside, praying and believing that life would come back to her. One thing that was difficult for Angie to wrap her mind around was the close relationship that Nicole had with several of her friends yet was always antagonistic toward her own sister. This caused Angie to feel rejected, adding to the myriad of other emotions she was experiencing about the fog of her sister's suicide.

Both Angie and her sister experienced chronic Asthma attacks that often kept them out of school. After the move, every time Angie attempted to attend school, she began to experience panic attacks that triggered her Asthma. She also began to have her own set of suicidal ideations. Her mother was just as tenacious as she was with Nikky in her efforts to get her support but was concerned that she was not getting better. She obtained support at her school from counselors, a private therapist, and a youth group that assisted with behavioral therapy. Her mother also solicited my services to provide Christian Life Coaching for Angie. My job was to help her with setting goals and to grow spiritually as she moved through her grief. We'd set goals whenever we had a telephone session, but when they were on their way to the airport for a Christmas trip with family, I was able to have a face-to-face session with Angie. It was at that point that I saw the impact of her sister's death and how deeply wounded Angie was. I had a conversation with her and pointed out that the key thing in all that is going on is that all of her goals in life have always been wrapped in some way around her sister. In light of this, I saw the need to shift from coaching, which is client-centered and goal-focused, to Pastoral Counseling in order to minister to her brokenness.

I realized that although it was not the exact same situation, it was similar to when I separated from my husband of 28 years, which was more than half of my life. I spent every waking day thinking about and maneuvering my life around this person. The goals I set always included him and considered him in some way. I shared with Angie that she, like me, with it just being 6 months after her sister's death, did not have the ability to realign her life apart from her sister. As I did, she needed to move through the grief and address the disappointment of every dream and vision that was shattered. I shared that in the Old Testament, they wore sackcloth and ashes when they were grieving. I shared that the ashes were symbolic of what remained after a devastatingly destructive fire and you are just sitting there with nothing left to pick up and put together. I assured her that God promised in His Word that He would give us beauty for ashes and she would one day experience joy again. I told her that she would live and not die to declare the works of the Lord because Jeremiah 29:11 states, *"For I know the plans I have for you."* **Declare** *the Lord.* **"Plans** *to prosper you and not to harm you, plans to give you hope and a future."* The following week, Angie had her best week ever because she was able to return to school. She shared with me that she began to read her Bible, and the story of Job helped her because he lost it all and still loved God. She talked about how excited and amazed she was by the life of God's Word and how real He is to her. Angie began experiencing psychosis and was thereby unavailable mentally for me to counsel. She had experienced several hospitalizations before finding the right combination of medications and becoming stable again. The psychosis and struggle to concentrate has made moving through school difficult for Angie, but she continues to work at it.

Father, I'm asking that You help those who have been impacted by suicide and remind them that earth has no sorrow that heaven cannot heal, and blessed are they that mourn, for they shall be comforted. I pray that they will know, without a doubt, that you are with them and still have a plan and good purpose for them apart from the person that they've lost. I thank you for answering this prayer in Jesus' name.

A Peaceful Fog

"Peace I leave with you; my peace I give you. I do not give to you as the world gives. Do not let your hearts be troubled and do not be afraid."
(John 14:27 NIV)

Until this point, we have uncovered the challenges that are produced through the fog of mental illness. The below devotional expresses the peace that exists within the fog. It speaks of the peace that comes from looking to God, and walking hand-in-hand with Him through it all. It expresses how the fog of your situation can become a tool that teaches you how to remain in the presence of God and focus on His bigness. You can become determined to talk to your problem about how big God is rather than talking to God about how big your problem is.

Jesus Calling Devotional

As you look at the day before you, you see a twisted, complicated path with branches going off in all directions. You wonder how you can possibly find your way through that maze. Then you remember the One who is with you always, holding you by your right hand. You recall My promise to guide you with My counsel, and you begin to relax. As you look again at the path ahead, you notice that a peaceful **fog** has settled over it, obscuring your view. You can see only a few steps in front of you, so you turn your attention more fully to Me and begin to enjoy My Presence.

The **fog** is a protection for you, calling you back into the present moment. Although I inhabit all of space and time, you can communicate with Me only here and now. Someday, the **fog** will no longer be necessary, for you will have learned to keep your focus on Me and on the path just ahead of you.

"Yet I am always with you; you hold me by my right hand. You guide me with your counsel, and afterward you will take me into glory"
(Psalm 73:23–24).

"Now we see but a poor reflection as in a mirror; then we shall see face to face. Now I know in part; then I shall know fully, even as I am fully known"
(1 Corinthians 13:12).

Self-Care

"All at once an angel touched him and said, "Get up and eat." He looked around, and there by his head was some bread baked over hot coals, and a jar of water. He ate and drank and then lay down again. The angel of the Lord came back a second time and touched him and said, "Get up and eat, for the journey is too much for you." So he got up and ate and drank. Strengthened by that food, he traveled forty days and forty nights until he reached Horeb, the mountain of God. There he went into a cave and spent the night."
(I Kings 19:5-9 NIV)

Adequate Rest: Rest is required to travel this journey, as sleep deprivation diminishes your ability to make sound decisions and process all that is transpiring.

Exercise: Exercise increases the endorphins in the brain which can combat depression. It also helps you to manage weight gain that can result from certain medications and emotional eating.

Smart Watches and Fitbits: These devices are great tools that monitor both your sleep and exercise habits. It shows patterns that help you evaluate when and what causes crisis. You can see how long you've slept and the quality of sleep that you have received with this tool.

Prayer: Prayer is communication with God, which is necessary to balance and bring all of your self-care efforts together. God is the Healer that causes all things to work together for our good. Prayer makes you sensitive to God's leading and open to His methods of healing.

Spiritual Growth: Studying God's Word increases our faith to walk in healing, and it helps us to know who we are in Christ in spite of the diagnosis. The Word of God holds the truth about what God says about every situation that we face in this life. Knowing God's Word and character helps you to differentiate between a manic idea, a depressive idea, and a God idea.

Therapy: Being a part of a therapeutic community helps to process behaviors related to the illness and monitor how well it is being managed. It is in the therapeutic relationship that changes in your mental status are easily identified and brought to resolution.

Medication: With neurochemical imbalances in the brain, medication is intended to bring the individual out of psychosis so that they are available for help through previously mentioned care approaches.

Support System: God always gives us someone who understands and can walk through life with us in every season of our lives. Do not allow the enemy to isolate you. The church may not know about your situation, but a healthy church is used by God to minister to our needs through corporate prayer, corporate worship, brotherly love, and preaching.

Finances: There are apps for smartphones such as "You Need a

Budget" that will help you track your money. Using cash as often as possible can help because when it is gone, it is gone unlike using bank and credit cards that can cause overspending and overdrafts.

Here are 10 Biblical Principles in the area of finance, to consider when experiencing manic episodes that can lead to unwise spending. They can also help you when recovering from decisions already made during a previous manic episode:

GOD IS SOURCE ... GIVE YOUR FIRST FRUIT TO GOD'S WORK ... LIVE WITHIN A MARGIN ... SAVE MONEY ... STAY OUT OF DEBT ... BE CONTENT WITH WHAT YOU HAVE ... KEEP RECORDS ... DON'T COSIGN ... WORK HARD AND SEEK GODLY COUNSEL.

Scriptures relative to finances:

"But my God shall supply all your need according to his riches in glory by Christ Jesus"
(Philippians 4:19).

"I lead in the way of righteousness, in the midst of the paths of judgment: That I may cause those that love me to inherit substance; and I will fill their treasures"
(Proverbs 8:20).

"And God [is] able to make all grace abound toward you; that ye, always having all sufficiency

in all [things], may abound to every good work: (As it is written, He hath dispersed abroad; he hath given to the poor: his righteousness remaineth forever. Now he that ministereth seed to the sower both minister bread for [your] food, and multiply your seed sown, and increase the fruits of your righteousness;) Being enriched in everything to all bountifulness, which causeth through us thanksgiving to God. For the administration of this service not only supplieth the want of the saints, but is abundant also by many thanksgivings unto God"
(2 Corinthians 9: 8–12)

"Give, and it shall be given unto you; good measure, pressed down, and shaken together, and running over, shall men give into your bosom. For with the same measure that ye mete withal it shall be measured to you again"
(Luke 6:38).

"Honour the LORD with thy substance, and with the firstfruits of all thine increase: So shall thy barns be filled with plenty, and thy presses shall burst out with new wine"
(Proverbs 3:9).

"[There is] treasure to be desired and oil in the dwelling of the wise; but a foolish man spendeth it up"

(Proverbs 21:20).
"A prudent [man] foreseeth the evil, and hideth
himself: but the simple pass on, and are punished"
(Proverbs 22:3).

"The wicked borroweth, and payeth not again: but
the righteous sheweth mercy, and giveth"
(Psalm 37:21).

"The rich ruleth over the poor, and the borrower
[is] servant to the lender ... He that hath a
bountiful eye shall be blessed; for he giveth of his
bread to the poor"
(Proverbs 22:7–9).

"[Let your] conversation [be] without
covetousness; [and be] content with such things as
ye have: for he hath said, I will never leave thee,
nor forsake thee. So that we may boldly say, The
Lord [is] my helper, and I will not fear what man
shall do unto me"
(Hebrews 13:5–6).

"Buy the truth, and sell [it] not; [also] wisdom,
and instruction, and understanding. The father of
the righteous shall greatly rejoice: and he that
begetteth a wise [child] shall have joy of him. Thy
father and thy mother shall be glad, and she that
bare thee shall rejoice. My son, give me thine
heart, and let thine eyes observe my ways"

(Proverbs 23:23–26).
"Through wisdom is an house builded; and by understanding it is established: And by knowledge shall the chambers be filled with all precious and pleasant riches. A wise man [is] strong; yea, a man of knowledge increaseth strength. For by wise counsel thou shalt make thy war: and in multitude of counsellors [there is] safety"
(Proverbs 24:3–6).

"He that tilleth his land shall have plenty of bread: but he that followeth after vain [persons] shall have poverty enough. A faithful man shall abound with blessings: but he that maketh haste to be rich shall not be innocent"
(Proverbs 28:19-20).

"In all labour there is profit: but the talk of the lips [tendeth] only to penury. The crown of the wise [is] their riches: [but] the foolishness of fools [is] folly"
(Proverbs 14:23–24).

"Without counsel purposes are disappointed: but in the multitude of counsellors they are established"
(Proverbs 15:22).

"Blessed [is] the man that walketh not in the counsel of the ungodly, nor standeth in the way of sinners, nor sitteth in the seat of the scornful. But his delight [is] in the law of the LORD; and in his law doth he meditate day and night. And he shall be like a tree planted by the rivers of water, that bringeth forth his fruit in his season; his leaf also shall not wither; and whatsoever he doeth shall prosper"
(Psalms 1:1−3).

Electronics: Spending an enormous amount of time using electronics or engaging in social media can cause overload. We are living in a time when we are not allowing our minds to shut down and rest. We are bombarded with advertisements that are designed to make us feel like what we have does not measure up. This leads to low self-esteem, overspending, anger, and more. It is also important to shut down electronics an hour before going to bed for a better chance at a good night's sleep.

Holidays: These are supposed to be times when families and others joyfully come together to celebrate, but most often, because of a hurtful history with some individuals, these events bring on stress that further impacts the illness. At times, self-care may mean passing up an invitation to a holiday celebration. Holidays also highlight a lack of significant relationships and can lead to despair, which means that your therapy sessions may need to be more frequent. Letting someone know if you are in crisis and in need of additional support is vital.

Health Check

(Depression and Mania)

1. I do things slowly.
Not at all
Just a little
Somewhat
Moderately
Quite a lot
Very much

2. My future seems hopeless.
Not at all
Just a little
Somewhat
Moderately
Quite a lot
Very much

3. My mind has never been sharper.
Not at all
Just a little
Somewhat
Moderately
Quite a lot
Very much

4. I need less sleep than usual.

Not at all

Just a little

Somewhat

Moderately

Quite a lot

Very much

5. It is hard for me to concentrate when reading.

Not at all

Just a little

Somewhat

Moderately

Quite a lot

Very much

6. The pleasure and joy has gone out of my life.

Not at all

Just a little

Somewhat

Moderately

Quite a lot

Very much

7. I have so many plans and new ideas that it is hard for me to work.

Not at all

Just a little

Somewhat

Moderately

Quite a lot

Very much

8. I feel a pressure to talk and talk and talk.
Not at all
Just a little
Somewhat
Moderately
Quite a lot
Very much

9. I have difficulty making decisions.
Not at all
Just a little
Somewhat
Moderately
Quite a lot
Very much

10. I have lost interest in aspects of life that was previously important to me.
Not at all
Just a little
Somewhat
Moderately
Quite a lot
Very much

11. I have been more active than usual.
Not at all
Just a little
Somewhat
Moderately
Quite a lot
Very much

12. I feel sad, blue, and unhappy.
Not at all
Just a little
Somewhat
Moderately
Quite a lot
Very much

13. I am agitated and keep moving around.
Not at all
Just a little
Somewhat
Moderately
Quite a lot
Very much

14. I talk so fast that people have a hard time keeping up with me.
Not at all
Just a little
Somewhat
Moderately
Quite a lot
Very much

15. I have more new ideas than I can handle.
Not at all
Just a little
Somewhat
Moderately
Quite a lot
Very much

16. I feel fatigued.
Not at all
Just a little
Somewhat
Moderately
Quite a lot
Very much

17. It takes great effort for me to do simple things.
Not at all
Just a little
Somewhat
Moderately
Quite a lot
Very much

18. I have been irritable.
Not at all
Just a little
Somewhat
Moderately
Quite a lot
Very much

19. I feel like a failure.
Not at all
Just a little
Somewhat
Moderately
Quite a lot
Very much

20. I have been feeling like "the life of the party."
Not at all
Just a little
Somewhat
Moderately
Quite a lot
Very much

21. I have been full of energy.
Not at all
Just a little
Somewhat
Moderately
Quite a lot
Very much

22. I feel lifeless—more dead than alive.
Not at all
Just a little
Somewhat
Moderately
Quite a lot
Very much

23. My sleep has been disturbed—too little, too much, or broken sleep.
Not at all
Just a little
Somewhat
Moderately
Quite a lot
Very much

24. I have been thinking about sex more often than not.

Not at all

Just a little

Somewhat

Moderately

Quite a lot

Very much

25. I have been feeling particularly playful during serious moments.

Not at all

Just a little

Somewhat

Moderately

Quite a lot

Very much

26. I spend time thinking about HOW I might kill myself.

Not at all

Just a little

Somewhat

Moderately

Quite a lot

Very much

27. I feel trapped or caught.

Not at all

Just a little

Somewhat

Moderately

Quite a lot

Very much

28. I have special plans for the world.
Not at all
Just a little
Somewhat
Moderately
Quite a lot
Very much

29. I have been spending too much money.
Not at all
Just a little
Somewhat
Moderately
Quite a lot
Very much

30. I feel depressed even when good things happen to me.
Not at all
Just a little
Somewhat
Moderately
Quite a lot
Very much

31. Without trying to change my diet, I have lost, or gained weight.
Not at all
Just a little
Somewhat
Moderately
Quite a lot
Very much

32. My attention keeps jumping from one idea to another.

Not at all

Just a little

Somewhat

Moderately

Quite a lot

Very much

33. I find it hard to slow down and stay in one place.

Not at all

Just a little

Somewhat

Moderately

Quite a lot

Very much

Conclusion

*"The silver is mine and the gold is mine,' declares
the Lord Almighty. 'The glory of this present
house will be greater than the glory of the former
house," says the Lord Almighty. "And in this place
I will grant peace," declares the Lord Almighty"*
— (Haggai 2:8-9 NIV)

As previously stated, I left the home we purchased, which I poured my love into, and my marriage of twenty-eight years because of the relational toxicity and mental cruelty. My daughter chose to stay, so my heart was terribly torn and saddened without her. I left for my own sanity, but I also left to be an example to my children. I wanted them to know two things: if they become an abuser, the person will eventually get the courage to leave them; and if they are being abused, they can step out on faith and trust God's love to walk them into the abundantly and healthy life that He purposed for them. It has been five years, and since that time, I have faced many arduous situations that required me to have an insurmountable amount of faith in God. At times, I did not know how I would meet my financial obligations or avoid an irreversible mental collapse from the stress of it all. There were instances when I was on the brink of disaster and close to losing my mind. Praise God for the ministry of Pastor Dharius and Shameka Daniels who God has used to show me the principles of what healthy relationships should look like and how to live with purpose. I've had the love of my children, friends, family, and church family to cover me. Time and care heal all wounds; so, along with that support system, I have continued in counseling. I take a minimal amount of medication and supplements, exercise regularly and, above all, spend time daily with God in prayer and His Word.

While it was grievous to walk away from a twenty-eight-year-old relationship that I put all of my hopes and dreams in, the Word says that God will "provide for those who grieve in Zion—to bestow on them a crown of beauty instead of ashes, the oil of joy instead of mourning, and a garment of praise instead of a spirit of despair. They will be called oaks of righteousness, a planting of the Lord for the display of his splendor," (*Isaiah 61:3 NIV*). In order to get the beauty and praise, you have to embrace the lessons learned from the past and surrender the ashes as well as the spirit of despair. The past was meant to learn from and not to live in. "This is what the Lord says— he who made a way through the sea, a path through the mighty waters, who drew out the chariots and horses, the army and reinforcements together, and they lay there, never to rise again, extinguished, snuffed out like a wick: "Forget the former things; do not dwell on the past. See, I am doing a new thing! Now it springs up; do you not perceive it? I am making a way in the wilderness and streams in the wasteland," (*Isaiah 43:16–19*). Something new means it hasn't been done before. I now have a new job and income that is double what I was making when I departed that abusive relationship. I prayed three years ago for God to double my income, and in the past two years, it was done in ways I would've never imagined. It was truly exceedingly abundantly above what I could ask or think. When you ask God for restoration and increase, leave the method up to Him. I have a brand new vehicle, and God has also blessed me to live in a beautiful and peaceful two-bedroom condo. My daughter is happily married to a wonderful young man named

Terrell, and they have a beautiful baby girl named Sarai. My son has graduated from high school and is on a training course to play college basketball. Don't let your mistakes, illness, or anything from **YES**terday ruin your **YES** today. SAY YES TO GOD AND HIS METHOD OF HEALING! YOUR ATTITUDE (WAY OF THINKING) ABOUT MENTAL ILLNESS WILL DETERMINE YOUR APPROACH, AND YOUR APPROACH WILL DETERMINE SUCCESS OR FAILURE. No matter what you have walked through in the past; no matter the sadness, the loss, the failure, or oppression; with faith in God, YOU CAN MAKE IT THROUGH THE FOG TO VICTORY AND SUCCESS.

References

Holy Bible

DSM-IV

Warren, R. (2002). The purpose-driven life: What on earth am I here for? Grand Rapids, MI: Zondervan.

Redfield Jamison, Kay. (1995). An Unquiet Mind,. 1st edition NY: A. A. Knopf.

Young, Sarah (2004). Jesus Calling. Nashville, Tennessee: Thomas

Nelson; Special and Revised Edition.

Baugher, B., & Jordan, J. (2002). After suicide loss: Coping with your grief. Newcastle, WA: R. Baugher.

www.treatmentadvocacycenters.org

www.bipolarhome.org

Resources

www.nami.org

www.juliefast.com

www.bipolarhappens.com

www.Schizophrenia.com

NOTES

BIOGRAPHY

Lisa Frank is the founder of Lisa Frank's Empowerment Services. She has a Bachelor's Degree in Theology from The United Bible College & Seminary of Orlando, Florida. She is a Certified Christian Life Coach, Pastoral Counselor and Motivational Speaker with a crisis, grief, and loss niche. She volunteers yearly at Camp Erin Philadelphia for grieving children who have experienced significant losses. Lisa has been an addictions counselor for eighteen years and a nutrition counselor for many years. The counseling field has exposed her to a diversity of populations with people suffering from many forms of mental illness. Her mental health experience began in a residential halfway house for women and children recovering from drug and alcohol addictions, and it continued at such venues as methadone clinics, correctional facilities, family practices, and other rehabilitation centers. She has counseled and educated thousands of people, primarily women, through life's challenges. Lisa has lead people through the pain and devastation of addiction and other traumatic events in their lives to recovery. She is culturally sensitive and has studied abroad for extended periods in Madrid, Spain, and San Jose, Costa Rica. She currently works in the healthcare field coordinating volunteers and Pastoral Care. Lisa enjoys crocheting and reading, but her primary joy and calling in life is being a mother to her daughter, Jélissa; son, Oscar; and grandmother to Sarai.

For

Invitations to Speak

Christian Life Coaching

Or

Pastoral Counseling Services

Contact Us

Website: www.coachlisafrankspeaks.com

Email: lisafrank@coachlisafrankspeaks.com

Mailing Address: P.O. Box 205, Marlton, NJ 08053

Telephone: 609-203-0724

Made in the USA
Columbia, SC
25 February 2018